ADVANCE PRAISE FO...

Be Your Customer's Hero

"Based on personal experience, Adam Toporek speaks to frontline staff and fills a void for them with this easy-to-read, relevant, and relatable guidebook. *Be Your Customer's Hero* is comprehensive, covering every angle imaginable to help employees better understand customers and empathize with them, all in the name of delivering a great experience. The book is crammed full of practical advice that they can use every day—and will want to refer back to often."

—Annette Franz, Founder, CX Journey

"In *Be Your Customer's Hero*, Adam Toporek has created a transformative book that shows customer-facing professionals not just how to deliver exceptional customer service, but why they should want to. For organizations with a disconnect between service strategy and execution in the field, Adam's book is a fantastic roadmap."

—Keith Pepper, VP, Client Development, StellaService

"In many customer service situations, a gap exists between what is a routine transaction and what could be a memorable experience. *Be Your Customer's Hero* will help close that gap."

—Steve Curtin, author of *Delight Your Customers*

"Having worked with numerous national franchise brands and now leading my own, I've seen how franchise owners struggle to get their frontline teams to deliver great service consistently. Adam Toporek has created a book that will help everyone, from unit operators to franchise leadership, bridge the disconnect between the training manual and the service floor—a book that will both motivate employees to want to deliver great customer experiences and show them how. For franchise operators, this is the perfect training-in-a-box for their business-in-a-box."

—David Long, Cofounder and CEO, Orangetheory Fitness

"*Be Your Customer's Hero* offers organizations the perfect tool to ensure that their customer experiences live up to their brand messaging. The book's power comes not only from its clear, no-fluff presentation of techniques, but also from its unique focus on mindset and emotion. It helps customer-facing professionals understand that working with customers is first and foremost a mental game, and then shows them how that game can be won."

—Graeme Newell, President, 602 Communications

"*Be Your Customer's Hero* is the *Swim with the Sharks* of customer service books! Over 80 quick-to-read chapters are stuffed with tasty how-to morsels for everyone on the front line and in the C-Suite. If you want to build a customer centered culture, this book will help get you there fast."

—Chuck Wall, author of *Customer CEO:*
How to Profit from the Power of Your Customers

"Relationships in business aren't created in the C-Suite. They are born out of the interactions between your customers and front line staff. *Be Your Customer's Hero* provides the easily digestible techniques your teams will need to bridge the gap between transactional service and building customer relationships for life."

—Stan Phelps, Founder of 9 INCH marketing,
author of The Goldfish Trilogy

"*Be Your Customer's Hero* is a valuable handbook for businesses that want to establish unbreakable bonds with customers. For twenty years, we have built a high volume business whose success has depended on building and maintaining strong customer relationships. This book is an excellent tool to help us take those relationships to the next level. I intend to make it required reading for all of our customer service team members."

—Joel B. Turry, President,
wordZXpressed Transcription Services, Inc.

"Whether you're working on the front line of a retailer, restaurant, hotel, or airline, *Be Your Customer's Hero* will make your customers happier, make you happier, and help you make a difference!"

—Mike Wittenstein, Managing Principal, Storyminers

Be Your Customer's Hero

Real-World Tips & Techniques for the Service Front Lines

ADAM TOPOREK

AMACOM
American Management Association
New York • Atlanta • Brussels • Chicago • Mexico City • San Francisco
Shanghai • Tokyo • Toronto • Washington, D.C.

Bulk discounts available. For details visit:
www.amacombooks.org/go/specialsales
Or contact special sales:
Phone: 800-250-5308
Email: specialsls@amanet.org
View all the AMACOM titles at: www.amacombooks.org
American Management Association: www.amanet.org

This publication is designed to provide accurate and authoritative information in regard to the subject matter covered. It is sold with the understanding that the publisher is not engaged in rendering legal, accounting, or other professional service. If legal advice or other expert assistance is required, the services of a competent professional person should be sought.

Customers That Stick™ and Hero-Class™ are trademarks of CTS Service Solutions, LLC.

Toporek, Adam.
   Be your customer's hero : real-world tips & techniques for the service front lines / Adam Toporek.
      pages cm
   Includes index.
   ISBN 978-0-8144-4905-9 (pbk.) – ISBN 978-0-8144-4906-6 (ebook) 1. Customer services. 2. Customer relations. 3. Management. I. Title.
   HF5415.5.T664 2015
   658.8'12–dc23
                          2014045798

About AMA
American Management Association (www.amanet.org) is a world leader in talent development, advancing the skills of individuals to drive business success. Our mission is to support the goals of individuals and organizations through a complete range of products and services, including classroom and virtual seminars, webcasts, webinars, podcasts, conferences, corporate and government solutions, business books, and research. AMA's approach to improving performance combines experiential learning—learning through doing—with opportunities for ongoing professional growth at every step of one's career journey.

Printing number

10 9 8 7 6 5 4 3 2 1

To my parents, Sharon and Eddie Toporek.
For teaching me at a young age the importance of
valuing customers—and for being the best parents
anyone could have.

Contents

Acknowledgments

Writing is a solitary endeavor, but producing a book requires the efforts of a team. This book could not have come into existence without the hard work and contributions of a number of wonderful people.

To my wife, Renee: Your patience and support these past years have been beyond compare, and my public appreciation cannot even begin to capture my private gratitude. Your devotion means the world to me. Without you, none of this would have been possible.

To my agent, Jeff Herman: You took a chance on a first-time author and made this book happen. I thank you wholeheartedly.

To my editor, Bob Nirkind: Your wisdom and understanding, insight and open-mindedness, made this process incredibly rewarding and this book infinitely better. Those who say the traditional publishing model brings little to the table have never had the opportunity to work with an editor like you. Many thanks to the rest of the team at AMACOM as well. Erika Spelman, Rosemary Carlough, Irene Majuk, and Janet Pagano—I appreciate all of your support.

To Donna Gurnic: Your dedication and hard work helped turn a fledgling proposal into a polished pitch and then into a published book. I will always be grateful for your faith in me and your enthusiasm for this project.

To Eunice Flores: You wore many hats to help this book become a finished product—research assistant, pre-editor, and focus group of one. Your frontline viewpoint made this book better than it ever could have been without you, and I appreciate all of your efforts.

To the team at Don't Panic Management—Becca Euliss, Tricia Keels, and Jess Ostroff. Thank you for all you do and for keeping the social and content train on the tracks.

To the friends, colleagues, and readers who touched this book in ways both big and small—Shonali Burke, Steve Curtin, Gini Dietrich, Deb Englander, Erin Feldman, Annette Franz, Dave Long, Graeme Newell, Keith Pepper, Stan Phelps, Jeff Toister, Joel Turry, Jeannie Walters, and Mike Wittenstein. Your impact is certainly greater than your mentioning here does justice to. Also, a special shout-out goes to Chuck Wall for the conversation on publishing that inspired the next-day epiphany that was the genesis of this book.

To all of the readers of the Customers That Stick blog and The Customer Conversation newsletter. Thank you for your continued fellowship and support. You make it all worthwhile.

And finally, to all of the customer-facing professionals and customers I've interacted with over the years. To all of those I've worked with and worked for, whom I've led and been led by, and whom I've served and been served by—I've learned from you all in one way or another, and for that I thank you.

Introduction

I wrote *Be Your Customer's Hero* for one reason: It's the book I wish I'd had during my years of owning and running retail service businesses. I'd always wanted something that showed frontline employees not just what they needed to know to be competent at customer service but what they needed to know to be great at it. I wanted a book that was easy to read and spoke realistically about the challenges they faced, that would help them take charge of their own mindset and better understand the mindset of their customers, and that would serve as both an instruction manual and a reference manual. In short, I wanted a book that would prepare my frontline employees for the difficult, unclear situations that often present themselves in the real world of customer service. *Be Your Customer's Hero* is that book.

This book is about the reality you face at work every day, where even your best customers can be complicated, irrational, and easy to disappoint. Where you can deliver perfectly and still not meet the customer's ever-shifting expectations. Where you have policies to follow, forms that customers must sign, and problems created by departments you've never even spoken to. Where you can find yourself constrained by limited resources or facing difficult decisions because you aren't able to give the customer what she wants. And where you can sometimes find that customers are mean, are bullies, or are just plain crazy.

The techniques you'll discover in this book aren't magic, but they can be magical. Much of what you'll learn is based on my own experience working with customers and customer-facing teams, and it is extremely powerful. This book is not an academic exercise; it's designed to provide you with actionable tips and tactics you can use immediately. Take what works for you; discard what doesn't. No matter your experience level, you'll find ideas and approaches that can have a major impact on how you work with customers and that will make your job infinitely easier and less stressful.

Be Your Customer's Hero is designed not just to educate but to motivate. It covers frontline customer service from A to Z, from basics like smiling all the way to advanced techniques like using sales-closing tactics. If you've had any customer service training, you've likely learned some of this before. Yet there's a gap in the customer service world between what everyone knows and what they actually do. Even the best of us can fall into bad habits and need to be motivated to re-embrace the fundamentals.

This book is structured in 10 parts with short chapters. Each part focuses on a single topic you can explore to make yourself a better customer-facing professional. Parts One through Three deal with the mentality of customer service; they'll help you see inside your customer's head—and your own. Parts Four through Six present the skills you need to become great at frontline service; they focus on great teamwork, customer service basics, and communication skills. Parts Seven and Eight show you how to handle difficult situations and work with nightmare customers; they explore specific techniques you can use to succeed in the most challenging circumstances. Part Nine covers customer service on the digital front lines, and in Part Ten, you'll see how you can put together everything you've learned.

Out of necessity, the book is composed of short chapters. The only way to cover so much ground is to hit each topic hard and fast. Topics that could have had an entire part of the book dedicated to them are covered in a few pages. Topics that could easily have been discussed in a variety of different places are discussed in one spot. To tie these pieces together and to help you find the information you need, you'll find references to other chapters within many of the chapters of the book.

• • •

So what does it really mean to be your customer's hero?

First, forget everything you've read about over-the-top acts of service, the kinds of things that go viral on the Internet. Forget about airlines that buy an entire flight full of passengers holiday gifts or bank ATMs that spit out expensive, customized presents for their customers. These are publicity stunts, not customer service, and while I love it when companies do these outrageous things for customers, they have nothing to do with real-world, day-to-day service.

To be the customer's hero means one thing above all else: It means being there when the customer needs you and making your personal interaction with the customer as memorably positive as possible. At my customer experience workshop and consulting company, CTS Service Solutions, and on its Customers That Stick™ blog, we often discuss Hero-Class™ customer service. In keeping with this theme, you'll see terms like "Hero-Class™ rep" and "Hero-Class™ customer experience" throughout this book.[1] To be Hero-Class, or to be your customer's hero, simply means to be completely, obsessively focused on your customer and to make the effort to meet or exceed her expectations every time.

Perhaps this talk about being the customer's hero seems quaint, maybe even a bit disconnected from the real world I've promised to speak to you about. But I truly believe that, despite the challenges of working in a customer-facing position, the quality of your work experience will be shaped by you as much as by your environment. I have the greatest respect for those who work on the front lines with customers; many years ago, I worked many of those same front lines myself, as a telemarketer, behind the counter at a musical instruments retailer, and in the aisles at a large bookseller. Front-line service reps are some of the hardest-working and most under-appreciated people in business, and working with customers can sometimes be a thankless job. I wrote this book because it doesn't have to be. If you have the tools and techniques to create better experiences and to resolve issues more quickly, you'll find frontline service to be highly gratifying, and even fun. Of course, there will be bad days and even worse customers, but when you adopt a Hero-Class approach to customer service, your time on the front lines will become infinitely better.

Hopefully this book will give you the inspiration, confidence, and skills you need to become your customer's hero.

Note

1. Customers That Stick™ and Hero-Class™ are trademarks of CTS Service Solutions, LLC. To keep things informal, I am going to drop the use of the TM in the remainder of the book.

Before We Get Started

One of my primary goals for *Be Your Customer's Hero* is to make it accessible. For this reason, it's written in plain language and with a conversational tone. Business-speak is kept to a minimum, and the language of the customer-experience industry is used only as necessary. As you'll learn in Chapter 50, jargon is a wall between you and your customer, and I didn't want it to be a wall between you and this book. Not only will I try to avoid management terms like "cross-functional synergies" and "omnichannel alignment," but I'll also stay away from frontline slang terms like "in the weeds" and "line busting." Of course, not all industry terminology can be avoided, nor should it be. Below are some of the foundational terms used in this book that will help us make our time together more effective and ensure that we are all on the same page:

- **"Service rep," "customer-facing professional (CFP)," "frontline employee," "team member," "associate," "customer service rep," "sales rep," "sales associate," and similar.** These terms all represent you, the person on the front lines, and I'll use them interchangeably throughout the book.
- **"The counter," "the cash wrap," and the "register."** These all refer to the place you ring up your customer.
- **"The service floor."** This is another term for the sales floor, meaning the area where you interact with customers. Let the experts who write books on sales call it the sales floor. To us, it's the service floor.

- **"Touch point."** A touch point is any place the customer comes into contact with your organization. It could be an in-store purchase, a phone message, or an email—wherever the customer "touches" your company is a touch point.
- **"Pressure point."** I use this term to describe touch points that have a significant impact on the customer experience and stand out as important.
- **"Customer experience (CX)."** CX differs from customer service (CS) in that CX entails the entirety of the customer's interactions with the company. The television commercial that brought the customer in, the cleanliness of the parking lot, the email the customer received after her purchase— these are part of the customer experience. There's no consensus about where the line between CS and CX truly is, but the best way to look at it is that CX represents the customer's entire journey, whereas CS is what happens at specific points along the way.
- **"Company" and "organization."** While the service principles in this book can apply to all sorts of organizations, like non-profits, I'll primarily use the word "company."

A final note. Many terms used in this book will vary in meaning among different companies and industries, and in some cases, a definitive name might not even exist. Don't get too caught up in the semantics; we've established enough common vocabulary that we can communicate, and that's all we need to jump right into Part One.

GREAT SERVICE IS ALL IN YOUR HEAD

CHAPTER 1

The Customer Is Always _____

Let's start with a quiz. It's a simple one. Just fill in the blank in the chapter title. If you've worked in customer service, one word will almost certainly come to mind to complete the phrase. It's the phrase that has been drilled into our heads, for better or worse, since our first exposure to customer service.

And let's be real—none of us are particularly fond of it.

At a recent conference, I struck up a conversation with a front-line service rep. When I mentioned that I was writing a book on customer service, the first words out of his mouth were, "What do you think of the saying, '*The customer is always right*'?"

"I think it's ridiculous," I replied.

He smiled, and then gave me a good-natured slap on the back. "I'm with you, buddy. You should see some of the customers I deal with."

"*The customer is always right*" is perhaps the most repeated and hated phrase in all of customer service. Taken literally, the idea is a joke. Customers are not always right; in fact, they're often so wrong that you wonder what they're even talking about.

Yet the focus on the literal meaning of the phrase has overshadowed the original intent of the idea: putting the customer first above almost everything else. The phrase was designed a long time ago to shift the mindset of service reps from taking advantage of customers to taking care of customers, from giving attitude to giving respect. At the heart of the phrase's deeper message is a fundamental truth of customer service, one that you must embrace if you're going to succeed in a customer-facing role:

You and the customer are not on equal terms.

Businesses exist to serve customers, and as a customer-facing professional, you're on the front lines of that service. You're the one who shows the customer every day how much your organization values him. Through your demeanor, your words, and your actions, you demonstrate the difference between you and the customer— that you're there to serve him and even to understand him, when he's under no obligation to extend you the same courtesy.

For instance, to deliver effective customer care, you need to understand that you don't know what's going on in your customers' lives. While most customers will never mention their personal issues when transacting business with you, your customer wants you to implicitly understand that her dog just died, that she was just diagnosed with an illness, or that she just received an eviction notice. Your customer expects your empathy, and you have to give it knowing that you might not get the same in return.

Sure, we all wish our customers would understand that two employees got the flu, one went into labor, and one quit without notice—all on Monday—and that's why the order did not go out on time. Or that our small business runs on a discount web host for $10 a month, and when that host went down, the key email we were sending on their behalf disappeared into the cyberabyss. Or that our multinational company's computer system is an amazing tool that successfully handles a million transactions a day, but that our local office cannot customize it for their needs. Of course, we wish that our customers understood that things happen, but that's not how the relationship works.

One of the first steps in adopting a great customer service mindset is embracing the idea that the customer relationship is not an equal one, that we're there to serve the customer and not the inverse. As customer-facing professionals, it's our responsibility to overcome our natural inclination to expect fairness and disabuse ourselves of the notion that the customer is expected to treat us the same way we treat her.

Now, this doesn't mean that the relationship is one way all the time. Customers have responsibilities too. Nor does it mean that the customer is exempted from the basics of human decency. What it does mean is that the relationship is not equal. We're there to serve the customer, and the responsibility for the relationship is on us.

You see, I don't think the customer is always right, but I do think the customer is always my top priority. And if you begin with that idea in mind, then you're on the way to delivering Hero-Class customer service.

CHAPTER 2

Winning Is Not a Customer Service Goal

The furor all began when a family of five tried to return home to England from Spain. They neglected to preprint their boarding passes, and when they arrived at the airport for their flight home, Irish airline Ryanair charged them 300 euros (about $380) in fees before allowing them to board. Unfortunately for Ryanair, the mother posted their experience to Facebook, and it went viral, generating around a half million likes.

Ryanair's chief executive officer, Michael O'Leary, felt compelled to respond. "We think Mrs. McLeod should pay 60 euros for being so stupid." he said. "She wrote to me last week asking for compensation and a gesture of goodwill. To which we have replied, politely but firmly, thank you Mrs. McLeod but it was your ****-up."[1]

O'Leary went even further, characterizing the woman and anyone else who doesn't print out boarding passes in advance as "idiots." He later backtracked slightly, explaining to the *Irish Independent* newspaper, "I was not calling her stupid, but all those passengers are stupid who think we will change our policies or our fees."[2]

Unfortunately, O'Leary's comments reinforce the stereotype that businesses and customers are at war and that businesses, particularly large ones, are willing to step on their customers if it will create a nickel more in profits. However, this stereotype is not true for most businesses.

Having been involved in a number of businesses throughout my life and studying businesses both big and small, I can tell you that "screwing the customer" is not what drives most businesses. Are the majority of businesses looking for ways to be more profitable? Of course. Are most looking for ways to get the maximum out of each transaction? Absolutely. But those objectives do not necessarily equate to a negative result for the customer. You can be more profitable by being more efficient. You can maximize transactions by selling customers other products or services that add value to their lives. Businesses can provide value to customers and receive value in return without trying to squeeze the customer for every possible advantage.

Sure, there are companies out there that view their customers as marks, objects in a game in which the objective is to take as much as possible and give as little as possible. These companies consider business a zero-sum game. In every interaction, someone wins and someone loses. If you look at the great companies that you admire, you'll find that none of them view their customers this way. Customer service leaders like Nordstrom or Amazon have a "relational view" of customers, not a "transactional view." (In the customer experience sphere, these terms are often used slightly differently and can be time based instead of viewpoint based.)

The transactional view of customers is what gives business such a bad reputation and results in expressions like "churn and burn." With a transactional approach, businesses seek to get the most out of each sale, no matter what the impact on the customer. They take the customer's money and then in essence say "Next victim," just like the cook at my elementary school used to say (if you ate his food you'd know why). These companies don't care if they see the customer again or, at least, don't care enough to sacrifice any potential profit in the transaction.

In a relational approach, businesses still attempt to get the most out of each sale, but they do so within a framework where the relationship with the customer is a top priority. In a relational approach, you often sacrifice short-term profit for the long-term relationship.

It's important to note that working with a relational approach does not mean you do everything a customer requests. Each organization will have its own limits on where to draw the line in each situation. For instance, most organizations would probably not honor the special pricing from a Memorial Day sale in August.

The difference between a transactional approach and a relational approach is simple: Transactional companies always place the line where it extracts the most money from the customer; relational companies look at the relationship and try to find a healthy balance.

This book is for those who believe in a relational approach to customers. If you're focused on a transactional outlook, I can't help you. You need a different book.

As you read the chapters that follow, bear in mind that your goal is not to win, not to get one over on your customers. Your goal is to create a healthy, profitable long-term relationship with customers that provides value to both parties.

The only winning that works in customer service is win-win.

Notes

1. Oliver Smith, "Ryanair Boss Slams 'Idiot' Who Forgot Boarding Pass," *Telegraph,* September 5, 2012, http://www.telegraph.co.uk/travel/travelnews/9522191/Ryanair-boss-slams-idiot-who-forgot-boarding-pass.html. Accessed September 23, 2014.

2. Charlie Weston, "O'Leary Denies Calling Woman 'Stupid' in Boarding-Pass Row," *Irish Independent,* September 6, 2012, http://www.independent.ie/irish-news/oleary-denies-calling-woman-stupid-in-boardingpass-row-26895014.html. Accessed September 23, 2014.

CHAPTER 3

Do You Know Your Mental Rules?

Like it or not, we all have rules about how other people should act. These rules begin as beliefs, as conscious and sometimes subconscious ideas about how people should behave. Over time, these beliefs can become something more than just what we think; they can become our framework for judging other people. To others they might just be our opinions, but to us they are hard-and-fast rules.

In his book *Awaken the Giant Within*, personal development legend Tony Robbins devotes an entire chapter to the concept of these rules. As Robbins says, "[W]hat will determine our emotions and behaviors is our beliefs about what is good and what is bad, what we should do and what we must do. These precise standards and criteria are what I've labeled *rules*. Rules are the trigger for any pain or pleasure you feel in your nervous system at any moment."[1]

When you're upset with someone for behaving a certain way, inevitably it's because that person violated one of your rules about how people should act. Most of us have too many rules, and our personal rules can be some of our greatest sources of conflict and unhappiness. One of the best ways I know to be happier in life and in business (including customer service) is to rid yourself of as many arbitrary rules as you can.

So what are some of the rules you hear on the front lines?

- I hate it when customers walk around the store on their cell phones.
- It drives me crazy when Jenny helps customers five minutes before close, and I get stuck emptying the trash.
- I can't stand when a customer asks me 50 questions when she can see I have multiple people on hold.

What is the common theme in the list above? They are all versions of "*I get upset when* ____ *happens.*"

I know a person who has much stronger rules about how people should behave than I do. Mall employees, people in traffic, family members—someone is often violating one of his rules. I'd venture to say that I have more professional stress and work more hours than this person, yet by all evidence, I seem to be much happier with my daily life. Why? I spend much less of my time being upset about what other people do or don't do.

This doesn't mean that every rule you have is a bad one. I think most service reps would be upset if a customer picked up merchandise off a counter and then dropped it on the floor when done with it. Some rules are understandable. However, many people have rules that diminish their lives instead of rules that enhance their lives. As Tony Robbins asks, "Do your rules empower or disempower you?"[2]

Look at your own rules. How many times a day or a week do you get upset about what someone on the service floor did or did not do, whether it's a customer or a colleague? Be honest. Then ask yourself this simple question: What affected my life more—what the person did or my reaction to it?

If you've got a lot of rules, I'll bet your reactions have had much more of an impact on your life than the actual actions themselves.

The next time you get upset with a customer or coworker, ask yourself why you're really upset. You might find that you have a rule or two that needs to be kicked to the curb. Because in customer service, and in life, the fewer rules you have concerning what other people should or should not do, the happier you'll be.

Notes

1. Anthony Robbins, *Awaken the Giant Within* (New York: Simon & Schuster, 1991), 373.
2. Ibid., 377.

CHAPTER 4

Be Proud, and Then Swallow Your Pride

In customer service, pride can be a double-edged sword. Pride in your organization can cause you and your teammates to go the extra mile. Pride in your organization's mission can cause you to want to help more people experience it. Pride in your work can cause you to always want to improve. The other kind of pride, however, pride of the don't-disrespect-me variety, can be poisonous in a customer-facing environment.

This sort of pride becomes a barrier between you and the customer. It can cause you to react unfavorably to a customer, to make it about your feelings instead of hers. When your personal reaction to a dissatisfied customer trumps your professional reaction, pride has won, and you and your organization have lost.

As much as we strive to proactively create great customer experiences, our organizations will on occasion fail our customers. Sometimes it happens because we have not delivered as promised, sometimes it happens due to circumstances beyond our control, and sometimes it happens because, even though we did everything right, our performance was not to the satisfaction of the customer. Try as we might to create Hero-Class customer experiences, there will always be times when we need to react to a dissatisfied customer. And it's in these circumstances that pride often becomes a challenge.

In my many years of working with employees and management in customer service, one of the biggest impediments I've seen to giving great customer service has been the professional's pride. From a psychological standpoint, most of us have been programmed to take reactions that are typical of upset customers as disrespect or rudeness (we'll discuss respect from the customer's perspective in

Part Two). Raised voices, sharp comments, angry ultimatums—all of these unpleasant interactions are part and parcel of serving customers, but they're also interactions that can provoke an undesirable subconscious response.

Upset customers will push your buttons on occasion (if you don't agree, then you've never been on the front lines), and it's your job as a customer-facing professional to control what happens when they do, to react as a person whose job it is to delight that individual and not as a person who needs to buoy her self-esteem by "winning" the argument. If you want to create a Hero-Class experience for your customers, then always remember that *unless you're the company's legal counsel, taking crap from customers is part of your job.*

And therein lies the challenge. These personal reactions we have are natural. Yet, part of what separates humans from animals is the ability to supplant instinctual reaction with conscious decision making. As a species, we're able to overcome our natural reactions and act within the context of a larger framework. As individuals, some of us are better at it than others.

The inability of some to depersonalize conflict behaviors is one reason I disagree with the assertion that anyone can be trained to be great at customer service. While I do believe that anyone who has the ability to be a good employee has the ability to deliver a great proactive customer experience, when it comes to reactive service, particularly issue resolution, not everyone is cut out for it.

Some people just aren't constituted to handle criticism and insults well. They cannot detach themselves, and they take customers' comments personally. They get their backs up, and being right becomes more important than winning customers over.

The role of pride in customer service is not talked about often because it's difficult to address. It requires helping customer-facing professionals overcome their programmed psychological reactions to certain stressors and helping them remain professional and calm in the midst of unpleasantness. You can't deliver Hero-Class customer service until you learn to swallow your pride and until you realize that, most of the time, the customer is not even angry with you personally, you just happen to be the one standing in front of him.

We'll discuss specific techniques for handling difficult situations and angry customers in Parts Seven and Eight. For now, simply think about how you react to tough situations and unpleasant customers. Think of how you can be proud of who you are and what you do without being so proud that you take customer frustration as a personal slight.

Now let's look at one of the greatest examples in history of a person who had to maintain his pride and swallow it at the same time: Jackie Robinson.

CHAPTER 5

Keep Your Cool When the Ball Comes at You

When World War II ended in 1945, Major League Baseball was still segregated along racial lines. Professional baseball players of African American descent played in a separate league from white players. In 1947, Branch Rickey, general manager of the Brooklyn Dodgers, made a bold move to change that fact. Rickey brought Jackie Robinson to the Dodgers, and Robinson became the first African American to play on a Major League Baseball team.

The story of integrating Major League Baseball is a complex one that has many layers, but there's no denying that a crucial part of the story is centered on one man: Jackie Robinson. Robinson was an excellent ballplayer—his career stats bear that out—but Rickey chose him not only because of his baseball skills but also because Rickey believed Robinson had the emotional skills to endure the terrible situations that were likely to face the first African American to cross the color line in baseball.

What does Robinson's story have to do with frontline customer service? Nothing—and everything. As a society, we often try to improve ourselves by learning from those who have been in situations more extreme than most of us will ever experience. We learn from our presidents, even though most of us will never make decisions as important as theirs. We learn from our soldiers, even though most of us will never be in a firefight. We learn from our sports legends, even though most of us will never face such a high level of competition.

However, this sports legend is not Michael Jordan or Wayne Gretzky, and the lessons he has to offer us are not about diligent practice or skating to where the puck is going to be. Jackie Robinson's career provides an inspirational lesson about the power of emotional fortitude and self-control. Robinson's amazing journey shows us the levels of professionalism and self-discipline that can be achieved in even the most trying of circumstances.

Of course, we can't compare what Jackie Robinson went through with what we experience on the front lines of customer service. Having to handle an upset customer who's yelling at you because you don't have her favorite ice cream flavor is not quite the same as what Jackie Robinson experienced—to say the least. Yet just because our challenges are not as intense or extreme as Jackie Robinson's, let's not make the mistake of minimizing them. Life on the front lines can be rough sometimes.

If you work on the front lines long enough, eventually you'll run into some real ugliness. I've heard derogatory comments related to race, gender, and social status from customers. I've seen a grown man be so abusive toward young frontline females that he made them cry. And I've seen threats, both veiled and explicit. These extremes are the exception, though, not the rule. In frontline service, what you'll primarily be exposed to is frustration and anger that results in rudeness and unpleasantness.

Jackie Robinson, of course, had to take much worse. From racial epithets to death threats to pitches thrown at his head, Robinson endured constant verbal, psychological, and sometimes even physical attacks, only to step up to the plate time and again, having to keep his cool at every turn.

There's a powerful scene in the 2013 movie about Jackie Robinson, *42*, where the manager for the opposing team is yelling vile and terrible things at Robinson while he's at bat. Robinson does not react—publicly. He steps away from the plate and takes a deep breath, then resumes batting. Once he finishes, Robinson walks past the dugout and into the tunnel beneath the stadium. There, he loses it.

He begins screaming and smashing his baseball bat against the wall. Eventually, he crumbles to the ground, breaking down into tears. Jackie Robinson was not great because he didn't get angry, sad, or offended; he was great because he controlled these emotions in public.

You'll never undergo the consistently demeaning and despicable attacks that Jackie Robinson had to endure, and certainly not on such a large, national stage. His struggle was epic and historic, and he's a true American hero. He provides a lesson to us all about how to maintain self-control in the face of unpleasantness. He reminds us that when someone yells at us about something as inconsequential as a missing ice cream flavor, we don't have to react, we can respond coolly and calmly.

Fortunately, we don't have to take everything that is thrown at us like Robinson did. We're in a position to draw a line once a customer's anger gives way to abuse, a topic we will cover in Chapter 73. Still, the lessons of number 42 are important. Because even when we're able to draw a line with an abusive customer, we must maintain our self-control and draw that line in a calm and professional manner.

Working the front lines means stepping up to the plate again and again. Remember, you're going to take a wild pitch once in a while, and even a few that are thrown at your head on purpose. Take a deep breath and keep your cool. That's what marks the difference between someone who's good at customer service and someone who's great at it.

CHAPTER 6

Are You Renting Customers Space in Your Head?

One of my favorite ideas related to the psychological part of customer service is the concept of letting people "rent space" in your head. The idea is based on the premise that intense interactions, even if infrequent, tend to resonate more with us and tend to impact how we view our experiences.

If someone cuts you off in traffic, do you:

1. Shake your head but assume the person has something important going on?
2. Think the person a jerk but let the feeling pass as quickly as the incident did?
3. Get angry and stay angry, so that you're twice as mad when the next person does something to displease you?

If you chose answer three, that's a perfect example of allowing someone to rent space in your head.

Customers will push our buttons. We'll take offense, get angry, and even feel discouraged that someone could behave the way our customer just did. In Chapter 5, we discussed how important it is to maintain self-control and to react professionally when these interactions occur. Once the moment has passed, however, many service reps do something that's almost as damaging as reacting in the moment: They hold on to the experience emotionally.

You might be familiar with the adage *"Fool me once, shame on you; fool me twice, shame on me."* Most of us embrace this mindset to some degree, whether consciously or unconsciously. It's natural to latch onto these unpleasant experiences, to want to avoid experiencing the same pain and discomfort again. Unfortunately, this defense mechanism (which we'll discuss from the customer's viewpoint in Part Two) is not very discerning. Once it's in place, it tends to impact your approach to all customers, not just the ones who might be challenging to work with. When you allow your last difficult customer to take up residence in your mind, your next customer inevitably becomes an extension of that person. Your outlook becomes something similar to, *"Been fooled once, shame on me, but there's no way I'm getting fooled again."*

Beginning your customer interactions in a defensive mindset is no way to create Hero-Class customer experiences, so we have to find a way to get rid of the customers who are renting space in our head. We have to find a way to not let these events stick around once they're over and to make sure that prior difficult customers are long gone when we interact with the next customer. The best way to do that is to understand how they got in our heads in the first place.

Let's look at a hypothetical pattern from a customer-facing professional's job. What's the typical mixture of customers that professionals will run across? In my experience, for every 100 customers served, you might find:

- 15 will be amazing and brighten your day.
- 50 will be polite and pleasant to work with.
- 20 will be neutral and unmemorable.
- 10 will be irritated and a bit rude.
- 4 will be angry and unpleasant.
- 1 will be crazy and just a little scary.

Of course, every job is different and every set of 100 customers is different. We have bad weeks, and we have good weeks. Also, if your job is specifically issue resolution, such as a help desk or a customer service line, then you'll have a higher percentage of negative interactions.

The accuracy of the list is not the takeaway here; the takeaway is that if you really look at the customers you serve, the tough ones are usually a small portion of the whole. Look at the list again; we're at 85 percent before we even get to a negative customer of any kind. The challenge lies in the fact that the extreme circumstances tend to stand out in our mind, particularly the really tough cases that provoke an emotional response within us. They might not be that common, but these are the customers we allow to rent space in our head.

What does the list for your job look like? Assuming you're not in an issue-resolution position, how many truly crazy customers did you deal with in the last two weeks or months? How many truly angry customers? If you really think back on it, it was probably a tiny percentage of the total customers you served. Now look back on how you reacted to those customers. How many of them overstayed their welcome? How many did you allow to rent space in your head for a few hours, a few days, or even a few weeks? How did those customers affect your job performance and job satisfaction?

When you allow difficult customers to rent space in your head, they tend to take up space that could be used for more empowering customers—and worse, they tend to attract their own kind. It's a version of what's known in psychology as confirmation bias. The more negative customers you allow in, the more tend to show up, because they confirm the underlying belief that allowed them to make camp in your mind in the first place.

The decision to let negative or difficult customers rent space in your head is yours and yours alone. You can choose to move on, you can choose to transcend pettiness, and you can choose to simply let it go. Let your attitude toward customers be shaped by the majority of wonderful people who need your help, not by the few who throw your day off track.

Of one thing I'm certain: Once you kick these negative tenants out, you'll find that you like who comes to live in your head a lot better.

CHAPTER 7

It's True: Your Attitude Does Determine Your Altitude

We've spent the last six chapters looking at the mindset you need to deliver Hero-Class customer service. We've looked at how we view customers and complaints and how we deal with difficult interactions. There's a final ingredient that ties all of these disparate strands into a big unified bow, and that's your overall attitude—toward your organization, toward your coworkers, and toward your job.

Of all the business clichés I've heard in my life, few are truer than this one: *Your attitude determines your altitude.* One of the reasons this outlook is so powerful is because your attitude is one of the few things in life that you have complete control over. No matter what happens to you—bad luck, bad timing, or bad circumstances—the one thing you can control is how you respond to it.

Attitude is a fundamental driver of success because it impacts everything else. If you dwell on the unfairness of life, you won't be inspired to better yourself. If you have a negative outlook, you won't attract successful people to your life. If you always focus on what's wrong rather than what's right, you won't be motivated to do your best. Don't be fooled by the few jerks who have climbed the ladder of success with a terrible attitude. In most industries, they're the exception, not the rule.

If you ask me, your attitude is one of the most important determinants of your future.

A frontline manager of mine once came to me to express her concerns about an employee who was constantly complaining in the break room. Nothing, it seems, was ever right for this employee. I asked the manager a few questions to make sure the employee was not creating a hostile environment or impacting business operations. She wasn't—she was just an unhappy person who brought everyone in the break room down. I also asked if she had been like that since the beginning or if it was a recent change, as that might have indicated something had happened to change her attitude. She had been that way since shortly after she was hired, it turns out; it was just who she was.

I gave my manager a few tips to help mitigate this employee's impact on morale, but I also told her not to expect a miracle. The sad reality is that you can find people like this employee in most of the break rooms on Earth. If that's who she is, then 20 years from now she's going to have the same kind of job and be sitting in someone else's break room complaining that everything is wrong and never taking accountability for any of it. People like that never get anywhere in life, and they always blame others for it.

You never want to be that person.

The job you have might not be your dream job, but no matter what, it's an opportunity, and the best way for you to seize that opportunity is to be the person who's focused on making things better. Be the person who sees problems and offers solutions. Be the person who steps up when things go wrong. Be the person who changes the topic when someone won't stop complaining.

We all have problems at work, and at some point, everyone needs to gripe (a little). Complain to a friend, complain to a spouse, or, if you can do so professionally and constructively, complain to your manager. Be sure to remember, though, that complaints from customers can be gifts (as we'll discuss in Chapter 56), but complaints from coworkers are not.

Great customer experiences begin with a great attitude, but so does satisfaction and happiness at work. Attitude certainly isn't everything; skills and competence do matter. However, without a great attitude, these attributes are almost meaningless. Your attitude will determine your ability to serve customers, your ability to inspire others, and your ability to work your way up in your organization.

Your attitude truly does determine your altitude.

PART TWO

THE MIND OF THE MODERN CUSTOMER

CHAPTER **8**

Customers Have Mental Rules Too

In Chapter 3, I discussed the concept of our having mental rules—rigid guidelines we create in our own minds about how the world should be and how people should behave. Well, guess what? We're not the only ones who have them; our customers have mental rules too.

Mental rules are like customer expectations on steroids.

Obviously, the idea of customer *expectations* isn't new to customer service training, but the notion of mental *rules* provides a useful framework for understanding that the word *expectations* is sometimes not strong enough to represent how customers feel. Occasionally, the customer's view of what, when, and how something should happen is so strong and so fixed that when we fail to live up to it, we get an upset customer instead of just a disappointed customer.

In our interactions with customers, we're often faced with a gap between the level of a service failure as we see it and the intensity of the customer's reaction to that failure. We can't understand why the customer is so upset over what we perceive to be such a minor thing. It might be that they have personal issues going on (as we'll discuss in Chapter 12) or that we've pulled one of their service triggers (as we'll discuss in Part Three). But it might also be that we've violated one of their mental rules.

What types of rules might customers have?

- Any store where an employee doesn't greet me immediately when I walk in the door doesn't have a well-trained staff.
- Any business that has to call me back for my credit card information did not adequately protect it when I gave it to them the first time.
- Any employee who picks up the phone while checking me out at the register doesn't care about me as a customer.

Customers' mental rules can come from anywhere, and here's the part you're really going to love: Sometimes we create those rules for customers ourselves. Imagine that a customer is greeted by a member of the store's staff the first seven times he walks into your business. Now imagine that on his eighth visit he is not. By that eighth visit, the customer has developed an expectation that he will be greeted, and when it doesn't happen, it violates that expectation. Perhaps he notices the lack of greeting but shrugs it off as a lone occurrence. That represents an unmet expectation. But perhaps that lack of a greeting angers him, and he asks to see a manager when he finally encounters a service rep. That represents a violated rule.

If a customer has a reaction that seems disproportionate to the issue, keep in mind the concept of mental rules. When you think you failed to meet an *expectation*, the customer might think you violated a *rule*. And therein lies the difference between disappointed and upset.

CHAPTER 9

What's In It for Me?

What do our customers want when they conduct business with us? Each individual, of course, has different wants and desires, but almost all customers have one central question underlying their business interactions: *What's in it for me (WIIFM)?*

The concept of WIIFM is taught across disciplines in business—from sales to management to customer service. WIIFM encapsulates the idea that people want to know what they will get out of something; they want to know how they will benefit. Customers are no different. Before they offer you their attention and hand you their money, they want to know what's in it for them.

As a customer-facing professional, you should always keep this outlook in mind so you can better understand what customers are thinking. Whether you're having a first interaction with a customer or dealing with a sticky customer issue, customers are always going to be interested in what they're going to get out of the situation: *"What am I going to get if I sign this contract?" "What are they going to do for me to make up for the hassle they put me through?"*

Talking about WIIFM doesn't paint a pretty picture for those on the front lines, though. Viewed through the transactional/relational lens we discussed in Chapter 2, WIIFM presents us with a world in which customers are always transactional in their approaches to us. Every transaction is simply an opportunity to get the most gain possible from a company. Fortunately, for the vast majority of customers, this is not the case. Customers actually want other things from their relationships with us in addition to knowing what's in it for them.

Customers are not one-dimensional; they want more than simply what they can consciously quantify. Customers want to feel valued. Customers want to feel appreciated. Customers want to feel special. I hope you noticed the word *feel* in each of those sentences, because it's key. Customers are driven by both what they can get out of a relationship *and* how that relationship makes them feel. If you can remember how both of these dynamics play into your customers' perceptions of you and your organization, you'll be well on the way to building a successful relationship with those customers.

Unfortunately, there's a big roadblock you might encounter as you travel down this road, and it's the fact that all customers are irrational.

CHAPTER 10

All Customers Are Irrational

Now that you know what customers want, I'm going to let you in on a little secret:

Customers don't usually know what they want.

At this point, I'm sure I've got you scratching your head, so let me explain. The degree to which the subconscious mind influences how customers experience the world is astounding—even the smallest inputs can influence customer expectations and behavior. The simplest changes to the details of customer experience—to price, to store layout, to overhead music—can profoundly change how customers view their experiences with your organization.

In his book *Predictably Irrational*, Dan Ariely, professor of psychology and behavioral economics at Duke University, describes an experiment in which participants were asked to rearrange random words into sentences. One experiment tested the impact of the words by "priming the concept of the elderly, using words such as *Florida*, *bingo*, and *ancient*."[1] The real research was not about rearranging sentences, though, but about the impact those specific words would have on the participants' behaviors. The researchers measured how long it took the participants, all undergraduate students, to walk down the hallway as they left the building. "Sure enough," notes Ariely, "the participants in the experimental group were affected by the 'elderly' words: their walking speed was considerably slower than that of a control group who had not been primed."[2]

How does this dynamic apply to customers? Customers can pick up expectations from a variety of inputs: How they were spoken to by the service rep on their last visit. What their friend said about your business at lunch the day before. How clean the entryway is. This is why customers who have been happy for years can have a change in attitude after just a few bad experiences. It's not always rational.

On occasion, a customer will consciously analyze the situation and come to a rational and fair conclusion with a thought process like this: *"I've been doing business here for five years and have had over 200 experiences. My last two experiences have been with the same service rep, and they've both been bad. It looks like she might be a bad hire or have had poor training. Maybe I should let the manager know that she may have a problem."*

What's more common is that the two bad experiences will automatically become a trend in the customer's mind: *"Wow, the service here has really gone downhill. This place used to be so customer-friendly."*

Is it rational to come to that conclusion after two occurrences out of 200? No. But it's how customers sometimes think.

William J. Cusick wrote an entire book, *All Customers Are Irrational*, on the many ways customers are not rational. They include:

- Customers act before they consciously make a choice.
- Customers lie to themselves.
- Customers can't predict how they are going to act in the future.
- Customer behavior can be influenced by almost anything.
- Customers think in metaphors.
- Customers apply human characteristics to inanimate objects.
- Customers want products with every feature, then don't use most of them.
- Customers tell themselves stories.[3]

The list above is not exhaustive, but if you work in a customer-facing role at all, it's exhausting. The list is not meant to scare you but to give you a brief glimpse into some of the ways your customers think and process information. Understanding that customers don't always process information rationally can be a great lens not only for helping you depersonalize customer behavior but also for assisting you in handling service issues. As you'll see in later chapters, concepts taken from the idea of customer irrationality, like the idea of "priming" from the word study mentioned earlier, can be incorporated into customer service techniques with excellent results.

As Dan Ariely's book title indicates, customers might be irrational, but they are predictably irrational. By understanding the ways customers process and use information, customer-facing reps can use these same psychological processes to create better customer experiences. That means customer irrationality is not always a bad thing.

Notes

1. Dan Ariely, *Predictably Irrational* (New York: HarperCollins, 2008), 170.

2. Ibid., 171.

3. William J. Cusick, *All Customers Are Irrational* (New York: AMA-COM, 2009), 39–43.

CHAPTER 11

Everyone Is Rushed,
Everyone Is Stressed

If there's one thing you can depend on today, it's that people are stressed. The conveniences that are supposed to save us time—email, text messaging, mobile everything—leave us in a state of always being "on," and it wears us down. People from all walks of life have similar complaints:

- There aren't enough hours in the day.
- The phone never stops ringing.
- Social media is just another thing to keep track of.

I bet you can relate. But it's often easy to forget that our customers feel this way too, and that they often come to our businesses rushed, stressed, and not wanting anyone to make it worse.

In July 2013, a video of a customer in an Apple store in California went viral. The customer, who became known online as the Apple Store Lady, the Angry Apple Store Lady, and the Crazy Apple Store Lady, has a pretty bad moment. She's caught on video screaming at an Apple Store employee, "I was told by Apple Care that I could come in the store and get the part," and then slamming her hand down on her own baby stroller to emphasize her point.

What was incredibly interesting was not that this poor woman, while not being very nice, was unfortunate enough to have a very bad moment caught on video and uploaded to the Internet; what was interesting were some of the articles written about the incident. Of course, many articles engaged in typical train-wreck type coverage and focused on the Apple Store Lady's rather extreme reaction. Others, however, took a different approach. They concentrated on how the Apple Store Lady represented how we all feel as customers from time to time. Here were a few of the headlines:

- "Screaming Lady in an Apple Store Lives Out Your Inner Monologue"[1]
- ". . . Woman Screaming in an Apple Store Perfectly Captures How We've All Felt . . ."[2]
- "Angry Apple Store Lady's Meltdown Represents the Fury in All of Us"[3]

I don't know if the Apple Store Lady yells at service reps regularly or if she's generally a nice person who just snapped in this particular situation. Either way, it's obvious she felt that Apple had created a huge inconvenience for her. We can infer from the evidence in the video that she needed a part for an Apple product, and assuming she understood correctly, Apple Care support told her she could go to the store to get the part. She packed up her baby, drove all the way to the store, and was told by the rep at the Apple Store something different from what she expected.

If you've much experience on the front lines, you know that Apple Store Ladies are everywhere. In fact, this is how the majority of your customers come to you: rushed, stressed, and easily annoyed. So what can you, on the front lines, do with this information? How can you make your customer's day more pleasant and less stressful? The solution is simple in principle, though it can be complicated in practice:

Make your customers' experiences as hassle free as possible.

As a frontline employee, you might not have much control over the processes customers find to be a hassle, but often you do have ways to make these processes as painless as possible and, perhaps, even pleasant. Let's say that in your business every customer has to fill out Form 723, and your job is to make sure that happens. Are there parts of the form you can prefill for the customer? Can you send the form to the customer in advance so he can fill it out ahead of time? If you work in a clothing store, can you take the clothes to the dressing room for the customer? Can you offer to hold the clothes the customer is carrying at the front counter while she continues to shop?

These specific ideas are not important; they may or may not work in your particular situation. What's important is understanding that no matter what your position in your organization, there are always opportunities to make the customer's experience easier. If you look hard enough, you can always find ways to minimize the hassle factor for your customers. And if you do that, you can make sure that the customers on your service floor don't become Apple Store Ladies.

Notes

1. Caity Weaver, "Screaming Lady in an Apple Store Lives Out Your Inner Monologue," Gawker, July 23, 2013, http://gawker.com/screaming-lady-in-an-apple-store-lives-out-your-inner-m-886642382. Accessed September 23, 2014.

2. Ryan Broderick, "This Vine of a Woman Screaming in an Apple Store Perfectly Captures How We've All Felt in an Apple Store," BuzzFeed, July 23, 2013, http://www.buzzfeed.com/ryanhatesthis/this-vine-of-a-woman-screaming-in-an-apple-store-perfectly-c. Accessed September 23, 2014.

3. Madeleine Davies, "Angry Apple Store Lady's Meltdown Represents the Fury in All of Us," Jezebel, July 23, 2013, http://jezebel.com/angry-apple-store-ladys-meltdown-represents-the-fury-i-887032736. Accessed September 23, 2014.

CHAPTER **12**

You Don't Know Your Customer's Story

While practically all customers have in common lives that are too stressful and hassle filled, what they don't have in common is a set of similar circumstances in their personal lives. Your customers do not have the same story.

Imagine you work the front counter at a dry cleaner. A middle-aged lady comes in and asks to get next-day service on her suit. She's been an infrequent but loyal customer for many years, but unfortunately she missed the cutoff for next-day service by a half hour. You let her know that the quickest you can have the suit back is two days.

Much like the Apple Store Lady, she loses it. She begins ranting that she's been coming to your store for years yet this is how she's treated. She tells you she knows she's not your most important customer, but nonetheless when she finally needs you, you screw her over. She starts cursing and screaming, and the more you try to soothe her, the more worked up she becomes. She's never been a problem before, but now it's as if she's possessed. So you nod your head and use your customer service training to try to calm her, while thinking to yourself, "What a jerk!"

And she was. However, what if I told you that she's a widow with three kids and lost her job eight weeks ago? And that she's had no success finding a new job and is about to be evicted from her house? And that the suit is her only professional outfit, and the only decent job interview she's gotten since being laid off is tomorrow afternoon? How does this change your opinion?

If you're like most people, this knowledge affects how you view the customer. Does it excuse her behavior or how she treated you?

No. But doesn't the knowledge of what she's going through and why she's so upset shift your perspective a bit?

We rarely know what's going on in a customer's personal life. Perhaps she's sick, or a loved one is. Perhaps he's having financial difficulty, or going through a messy divorce. We all have challenging times in our lives. If you serve 100 people in a day, what are the chances that none of them are going through something really challenging in their personal lives? We don't know each customer's story, and it helps to remember this when you're trying to process why a customer is being less than nice to you.

I was first introduced to this idea decades ago when I read Stephen Covey's *7 Habits of Highly Effective People*. In that book, Covey shares a story about a subway ride he took:

> I remember one Sunday morning, on a subway in New York; people were sitting quietly. . . . Then suddenly, a man and his children entered the subway car.
>
> The children were so loud that instantly, the whole climate changed. . . . The children were yelling back and forth, throwing things. . . . I could not believe that he could be so insensitive as to leave his children like that. . . .
>
> I turned to him and said, "Sir, your children are really disturbing a lot of people . . ." [The man] said softly, "Oh, you're right, I guess I should do something . . . their mother died about an hour ago. I don't know what to do, and I guess they don't know how to handle it either."
>
> At that moment, my paradigm shifted. . . . Feelings of sympathy and compassion flowed freely. "Your wife has just died. . . . What can I do to help?" Everything changed in an instant.[1]

As Stephen Covey's great example demonstrates, every person— every customer—has a story. You never really know what's going on personally with someone who's at your counter. This concept, this alternative perspective, is not presented so you'll excuse bad behavior. We all have something going on (or multiple things going on) throughout our lives, and it's our duty as individuals and citizens to take responsibility for our actions and behaviors. This concept is presented to help you understand why some customers behave the way they do.

As a customer-facing professional, one of the best things you can do to enjoy your job and deliver Hero-Class customer service is to approach customers from the perspective that you don't know what is going on with them. This knowledge can help remind you that everyone who's short with you is not a jerk, everyone who ignores you is not rude, and everyone who curses at you is not a bully. This knowledge can help you keep in mind that most of the time it's not personal but really is about something else.

The customer has a personal story that can impact how he reacts to adverse situations with your organization, but the customer's story is not just about his personal life; it's also about his history engaging with your company and other companies. This means that your customer doesn't just bring his personal baggage with him when he walks through your door; he brings a history of bad experiences with other companies as well.

Notes

1. Stephen R. Covey, *The 7 Habits of Highly Effective People,* 25th ann. ed. (New York: Simon & Schuster, 2004), 38–39.

CHAPTER 13

Everyone's Been Burned Before

Let's face it: Every one of our customers has been burned before. Somewhere, somehow, sometime, an organization gave her a terrible customer experience—one where she felt abused, disrespected, and even taken advantage of. Most likely it's happened more than once.

As we discussed in Chapter 6, we can allow negative experiences with customers to camp out in our minds long after the experience has passed. Similarly, customers can hold on to the negative experiences they have had with businesses. In many cases, these bad experiences don't get erased from the customer's mind when they're over; instead, they leave lasting scars that eventually become defense mechanisms.

I also brought up the expression *"Fool me once, shame on you; fool me twice, shame on me"* in Chapter 6. That expression is but one of many that people have developed around this idea. The common phrases *"Once bitten, twice shy"* and *"Won't get fooled again"* show how this concept is an integral part of how many view the world. It emphasizes that people don't like to feel like fools and that they'll erect significant defenses to prevent that from happening. For customer-facing professionals, the bad news is that, in many cases, these defenses were created by someone else, somewhere else, but *you* have to deal with the results nonetheless.

In January 2012, I wrote a blog post titled "Why Your Awful Customer Service Sucks for Me." In that post, I wrote a letter to a fictional business owner whose business had provided such bad customer service that the customer had gone elsewhere. The letter discussed what it was like for my business to be the next to deal with that customer. What I said to that business owner in my hypothetical letter sums up how customers often react to bad experiences and the fallout those on the front lines can face:

> *"I should thank you for setting the bar so low that I barely have to raise my foot to step over it. . . . You've made looking good all too easy. So, maybe I should thank you. Then again—maybe not.*
>
> *"You see, while you would think that we would be able to shine by virtue of comparison to your [terrible] customer experience, looking for better is not the dominant mindset that your customers walk away with. When your customers come to me, they are usually not thinking 'anything is better than that last place,' when they come to me they are thinking 'how is this place going to try to screw me.' . . .*
>
> *"You've sent me a customer who is jaded, tired, defensive and ready to find conspiracies and malicious intent at the first sign of something going wrong. Actually, you haven't sent me a customer; you've sent me a victim of Post-Traumatic Shopping Disorder. It will take me months, maybe years, to gain this person's trust and to turn them into a profitable customer that does not need hand holding and reassurance at every step of the customer experience."*[1]

While the letter above is fictional, it captures how customers react to past negative experiences. They often come to us jaded and defensive. They've been burned before and have set up varying ways to avoid being burned again. Many of these defenses become automatic over time. Certain situations, certain communications can immediately trigger an unfavorable response from a customer. I call these stimuli service triggers, and I've identified seven of them that seem to most commonly affect customers. If you can understand these Seven Service Triggers, you'll be able to prevent a variety of common customer service issues from ever occurring.

Note

1. Adam Toporek, "Why Your Awful Customer Service Sucks for Me," January 31, 2012, http://customersthatstick.com/blog/uncategorized/ why-your-awful-customer-service-sucks-for-me/. Accessed October 27, 2014.

CHAPTER **14**

Introducing the Seven Service Triggers

The foundation of the Seven Service Triggers was built upon the idea that our customers do not come to us as a blank slate. Even if they are new to our business, they've had experiences with companies like ours before. And these experiences, for better or worse, have shaped their outlooks and reactions.

The concept of the Seven Service Triggers is not scientific, nor is it meant to be. It's a framework derived from my experience working directly with customers and frontline employees. In these interactions, I observed certain customer behavior patterns emerge. Specific situations seemed to be obvious triggers for customers, creating almost instantaneous negative reactions.

Why are these triggers so powerful? Because perhaps the two most powerful ideas you can combine in customer service are awareness and prevention. In customer service, the old cliché is true: An ounce of prevention is worth a pound of cure. The best way to handle a service issue is to prevent it from happening in the first place.

In Chapter 13, I discussed the idea that everyone's been burned before, and the metaphor of being burned is a useful one for understanding how the seven triggers develop in individuals. I remember that when I was around 10 or 11, I was in my grandfather's car, and like young kids do, I was messing around with the different buttons and gadgets. At one point I pushed in the cigarette lighter. When it popped out, the coil was glowing red, and I could feel the heat radiating from the coils with my other hand. After a few seconds, the coils stopped glowing, and my curiosity got the better of me. I pressed my thumb on the coil and burned myself pretty badly. What lesson did I learn? That I was an idiot—but also that a cigarette lighter does not need to be red to be hot.

Human beings are wired pretty simply: We look to find pleasure and to avoid pain. You touch a hot stove, and you immediately learn not to do it again. What many people seem to forget is that this mechanism does not apply only to physical pain but to things that cause us psychological discomfort as well. For example, as a child you may have known someone who was not very nice to you and would always stare when he was being mean, so you learned to associate anything more than brief direct eye contact as aggressive and unpleasant. Years later, you still take direct eye contact as an act of disrespect and aggression instead of as an act of respect and attention.

The same thing happens with our customers. They have had bad experiences, frustrating experiences, even maddening experiences, and these experiences often stay with them long after they have ended. Customers make a variety of associations around their experiences. They learn that being transferred means starting over. They learn that when employees disengage, they don't come back. They learn that a lack of eye contact means a service rep doesn't care. Whether grounded in reality or not, customers eventually associate certain actions with certain meanings, and like any mental association, specific circumstances can stimulate these associations. Just as a certain smell or song can make you feel happy because you have associated it with a good time in your life, specific situations that customers encounter will often trigger negative associations from their previous experiences.

The most common of these situations are the Seven Service Triggers:

1. Being ignored
2. Being abandoned

3. Being hassled

4. Being faced with incompetence

5. Being shuffled

6. Being powerless

7. Being disrespected

The goal of understanding these triggers is to identify them ahead of time and to use the techniques and strategies I'm going to show you to avoid having them be pulled in the first place.

At first blush, what you might notice about the Seven Service Triggers is that they do not exist in a vacuum. Many of them overlap. If a customer feels he is being ignored, he may feel disrespected as well. If a customer feels she has been abandoned, she may also feel powerless.

The triggers do not apply equally to everyone. One person's hot button is another person's no big deal. The level of reaction differs as well. On one extreme is the Zen-like person who you basically have to throw staplers at to provoke into an adverse reaction. On the other extreme is the hair-trigger person who reacts to even the most minor inconvenience as a major cataclysm. The great majority fall somewhere in between.

In the chapters that follow, we will explore the Seven Service Triggers in detail—what they are, how to identify them, and specific techniques for preventing them from being pulled. You will find common themes, such as awareness and prevention, woven throughout these chapters. You will also find common techniques that work across multiple triggers. In fact, the overlap is so great between Service Trigger #1, Being Ignored, and Service Trigger #2, Being Abandoned, that I have dedicated a separate chapter for techniques pertaining to these two.

So far we've laid the conceptual groundwork to provide you a foundation for delivering Hero-Class customer service. You've learned about your own mental game and about the mind of the modern customer. Now it's time to start diving into some of the real-world techniques you can use on the front lines.

CHAPTER 15

Service Trigger #1: Being Ignored

Have you ever:

- Walked around a department store and had no one approach you?
- Rushed into a restaurant and had no one assist you?
- Stood at a service counter and had employees ignore you?

As customers, we all know the frustration of going into a business only to find that no one cares enough to pay attention to us. Our customers have had these same experiences as well: sales reps who were more concerned with texting than working, waiters who took 15-minute smoke breaks in the middle of the meal, and all manner of apathetic and uncaring service (un)professionals. As paying customers, we expect a certain amount of attention, a bare minimum at least—and that bare minimum is to not be ignored.

From the customer service side, this one seems easy, right? Just don't ignore anyone. If only it were that simple. As you might have guessed by now, every customer has a different idea of what it means to be ignored. They also have different ideas of what being ignored means in different circumstances.

So what's a customer-facing professional to do? While some of the causes of customers' being ignored are outside frontline control (the store being understaffed, for instance), most customers who feel ignored feel that way because of poor execution. The good news is that I will show you some simple actions you can take to make sure your customers rarely if ever feel ignored.

But before we get to those techniques in Chapter 17, let's look at Being Ignored's even more evil twin, Being Abandoned.

CHAPTER **16**

Service Trigger #2: Being Abandoned

One common fear most customers have is abandonment. No, they aren't worried a boyfriend or wife will leave them; they're worried you'll leave them. When a customer is in the midst of a transaction or a service issue, he wants the transaction completed or the problem solved—or to know that it will happen soon. Nothing undermines this belief like disconnecting from the customer, whether it is to pass the customer on to a different department or even to take time to research the issue.

As customers, we've all been burned too many times in this regard, abandoned by customer service reps in a multitude of different ways. We've been left to slog our way through phone-tree hell, told that someone would call us back who never did, or left with information that was supposed to fix our problem but didn't.

From a technical standpoint, being abandoned is similar to being ignored; the main difference is that the customer has already had contact with someone from the organization. The customer is in the midst of his experience, and suddenly he is disconnected from the organization. Here are a few typical examples of customers' being abandoned:

- A customer is left on hold for 10 minutes.
- A customer is left waiting at the counter for 15 minutes while someone checks the stockroom.
- A customer is told he will receive a call by close of business, and the call never comes.

Or the customer is simply forgotten altogether, which is what happened to a Louisiana boat captain named Tom Wagner.

Imagine falling asleep on an airplane and waking up to a plane that is dark and empty. That's what happened to Tom Wagner in 2013 during a layover in Houston. Tom fell asleep on a small ExpressJet flight from Louisiana to Los Angeles, and when he awoke he found out just how inattentive some airline personnel can be. He opened his eyes to find the plane empty and the doors locked. He was trapped.

Fortunately, Tom had his cell phone and was able to convince his girlfriend that he was not joking: Yes, he had actually been abandoned on an empty airplane! His girlfriend called United Airlines, the main carrier, and a representative replied to her inquiries by saying, "Ma'am, we sweep those planes. There's no way he's on that plane." Eventually, the girlfriend convinced United that Tom was indeed on the plane, and about a half hour later he was rescued. [1]

While Tom's story is extreme, less severe versions of his story happen every day. Whether it involves leaving them on hold or leaving them at the counter, service reps regularly abandon customers, and for most customers, it has happened far too many times. As a result, when it comes to customer service, everyone has abandonment issues.

If you've been in a customer-facing role for any amount of time, you've no doubt worked with a customer who has pressed you for every detail before allowing you to disconnect from her. *"Who will be calling me back? When can I expect a call? Who should I call if I don't hear from him?"* I've worked with those customers before; heck, I've *been* that customer before. This is exactly what a customer who has been abandoned before sounds like.

When approaching the issue of customer abandonment, the most important thing to remember is that the customer does not view time the same way you do. If you are sitting in the manager's office for 10 minutes working on the customer's problem, you are actively engaged in the issue. The customer, on the other hand, does not know that. He only knows that you are out of sight and that it is taking a very long time for you to return. Be mindful of this difference in perception as you focus on the techniques in the next chapter.

Notes

1 Scott Stump, "'Get Me off This Plane': Man Locked in Dark Cabin in Worst Layover Ever," CNBC, December 9, 2013, http://www.cnbc.com/id/101257219. Accessed September 23, 2014.

CHAPTER **17**

Avoiding Service Triggers #1 and #2

Making sure your customers don't feel ignored or abandoned begins with an awareness of their expectations, as well as a desire to proactively use this information to prevent issues from occurring. One of the first steps is putting yourself in their shoes. How is the customer viewing time? What are her expectations in the situation? Where in the experience does the customer want assistance? Once you understand what your customer expects at different points in her customer experience, then you can use specific techniques to help make sure she never feels ignored or abandoned.

Below are nine techniques that can help you preempt Service Triggers #1 and #2. These techniques are presented in an overview form so you can focus on the overall approach to them as an antidote to the service triggers. Some of these techniques are so useful in a variety of customer service situations that they need to be expanded on in more detail. Where techniques have been given their own chapters later in the book, it is noted in this list.

1. Know your industry. In every industry, customers have different expectations about contact and communication from service providers. If someone goes through the drive-through of a fast-food restaurant, pulls up to the speaker, and waits a full minute before a voice comes over the speaker, that customer will most likely feel ignored. On the other hand, if a customer sits down at a fine dining restaurant and a waiter does not appear within the first minute, the customer will not think twice about it.

Understanding the expectations customers have for your industry helps you know what the average customer expects. In a big-box store (i.e., a large retailer), a customer might not expect to talk to a service rep at all unless he needs help. In a small boutique, a customer might expect contact no matter what. Know what the expectations are for your industry, and then exceed them whenever possible.

2. Know your company. The expectations in your industry might be one thing, and the expectations set by your company might be another. Has your company set a service standard that is now a customer expectation? For instance, Domino's once had a 30-minutes-or-less delivery guarantee. This set an expectation as to when a pizza would arrive from Domino's. However, a local pizza parlor could easily have had a 45-to-60-minutes delivery window without upsetting customers if it made sure to set that expectation consistently. The companies were in the same industry but could still have established different expectations about delivery time.

3. Don't ignore a ringing phone or a chiming email. One way to make sure your customers feel ignored is to not respond to a ringing phone. How many rings are too many? That depends on your particular company, though anything past three is probably too much in most business-to-consumer industries. Whatever the standard is for your company, you should know it and observe it.

Email response times are more subjective. In any frontline role that involves the use of email, you should understand what your response times are to certain types of inquiries. Be sure you are aware of your company's public promises and your internal guidelines about email response times and always seek to exceed them. We will examine email customer service in more detail in Chapter 78.

4. Check in frequently. If your frontline work is in a call center, you probably have a defined set of rules and expectations about hold times and checking back in with customers. For most other frontline positions, the phone is a key touch point where customers often feel ignored or abandoned, particularly when placed on hold. When a customer is on hold, it's important to remember that customers perceive time differently than you do. Be aware of the time and check back in. You don't have to solve the problem; just let them know that you are still working on it.

Similarly, when you disconnect from customers on the service floor, they can also perceive time very differently. If you are in the back looking for a customer's size and it's taking a while, simply go back and check in with the customer. *"Ma'am, there's one more box I can check, but it's up on a pallet and it might take a little bit. Do you have another 10 minutes? If not, I can take your name and number and give you a call once I determine if we have the item."*

5. Use the 10-5 Rule. The 10-5 Rule states that if you are within 10 feet of a customer, you should make eye contact and smile; if you are within 5 feet, you should greet and assist. The rule has been around customer service forever. While it only truly applies to retail environments, it is a great framework for helping to make sure customers do not feel ignored. Don't get too hung up on the number of feet. If you work at a large home improvement store or a department store, 10-5 might be a good rule. If you work at a small clothing store, your rule might simply be to greet and assist whenever you make eye contact with a customer.

6. Be aware of the customers on your floor. Of all the ways to help customers not feel ignored, this one might be the most important. Simply being aware of what is happening on the service floor and learning how to read body language can help you ensure that customers do not feel ignored or abandoned. If you keep your eyes open, you can see which customers are content and which are growing impatient. Perhaps while you were helping one customer, you noticed another customer browsing for multiple minutes without anyone acknowledging him. That awareness will allow you to make contact with that customer or let another rep know he has not been helped yet.

7. Use BRWY communication. BRWY stands for "Be right with you." This type of acknowledgment is incredibly powerful in making sure that customers don't feel ignored. One of the most common areas where they often feel ignored is when service reps are tied up with other customers, either in person or on the phone. Just the mere act of acknowledging a customer briefly with a simple phrase like, "I'll be with you in a moment," can make a huge difference. I'll focus more on this potent technique in Chapter 47.

8. Get buy-in for your response time. This is one of my favorite techniques, and it's one that is rarely talked about. Here's how this works: When you have to disconnect from a customer, the tendency is to tell him something. *"I need to go check with my manager; I'll be back in a few minutes,"* Or, *"I have to check with the IT department supervisor; she's not in until Tuesday."* What's much more powerful is to get the customer to buy in to your response time. *"Ma'am, I need to check the storeroom; do you have five minutes for me to go look for that size?"* *"Sir, my manager is not in until morning; would you mind if we got back to you by the end of the day tomorrow?"* This is expectation setting on steroids, because it helps the customer feel like he has control over the process and softens the fact that you have to disconnect from him. For more on getting buy-in for your response time, see Chapter 53.

9. Assure accountability. This is an almost magical technique. Assuring accountability means you are taking ownership of the customer's issue and giving her assurance that someone is going to see it through to the end. Assuring accountability is particularly important when you have to transfer or elevate a service issue. It works like this: *"Sir, I'll have to connect with our IT department to look into this issue further; however, I'll personally follow up to make sure this situation is being worked on. Can you give me until Wednesday to get back to you with an answer?"* Assuring accountability is so effective because it preempts the conditioned response most customers have to being transferred—the fear that they will be abandoned in the process. I'll discuss some more specific ways to use this technique in Chapter 52.

If you employ the preceding techniques proactively and preemptively, they will help you become more effective at preventing two of the biggest service triggers of all. Now that your customers are no longer being ignored or abandoned, let's look at how they feel when your company pays attention to them, but not in a good way.

CHAPTER 18

Service Trigger #3: Being Hassled

If you recall from the Chapter 11, the pace of modern life has made the average customer stressed out and short on patience. Despite almost every time-saving measure and device created, few things in life are easier.

Modern life is full of hassles, and as a result, people are more sensitive than ever to companies that create hassles for them: *"You have to come to our office to fill out this form." "You must fax your records in; you can't email them." "Only our accounting department can get that information for you, and they don't work on Fridays."* Customer hassle, known more formally as customer effort, is a huge issue for companies and customers—and it's an important trigger to be aware of.

In their excellent book, *The Effortless Experience*, authors Matt Dixon, Nick Toman, and Rick Delisi put forth the proposition that an important driver of customer loyalty is how little effort the customer has to expend to do business with you. While this is not a new concept—the acronym ETDBW (easy to do business with) has been around for quite a while—the authors demonstrate through their research why it's more than just a slogan; it's an important philosophy that companies (and customer-facing professionals) should embrace.

One of the startling findings of the authors' research was that 96 percent of respondents who reported having high-effort experiences said they would be more disloyal in the future.[1] As a businessperson, when I hear that 96 percent of customers feel something is important, I pay attention. As a customer-facing professional, you should too.

We've already spoken about the principle of trying to make your customers' experiences as hassle free as possible. Now let's look at three specific ways you can make that happen:

1. Identify your customers' biggest hassles. The first step is to understand what your customers consider a hassle and what they don't. Some hassles are minor; some are major. Some hassles occur frequently; some hardly ever occur. Focus on the few hassles that occur most frequently and that cause the worst customer service issues. Think about the complaints you and your teammates receive on the front lines. You'll realize very quickly which touch points create the biggest hassles for customers. Once you identify the pressure points that result in high customer effort, begin looking for ways you can help customers have an easier experience at those critical junctures.

2. Know what flexibility and authority you have. One pattern I have noticed in working with frontline reps is that they are often unclear about what authority they have. *"I didn't know I was allowed to do that"* is a common refrain. Now that you've given some thought to the main hassles your customers experience, ask yourself what would make the situation better for them. Could you offer to email the customer the form you need to get from the back office so he doesn't have to wait? Are you allowed to do that? How easy would that be to accomplish? If you're not clear about what you can and can't do, talk to your manager. Most managers will appreciate your taking the time to understand the rules and to figure out what you can do to make your customer's experiences easier.

3. Know what your systems can do. It's not enough to know what you can do; you also need to know what your systems can do. I saw this principle in action on a recent trip to a frozen yogurt shop. The yogurt store is set up for self-service.

You pick from a variety of flavors and toppings, and then your cup is weighed at checkout. As I stood at the checkout counter waiting for my wife to finish making her cup, the counter rep offered to weigh my cup. I was concerned that other people might get to the counter before my wife and I would hold up the line, but the counter rep told me that it didn't matter—she could weigh my cup and save it in her system. This frozen yogurt chain had the systems in place so I didn't have to stand waiting at the counter, but the system was only effective because the counter rep knew how to use it and cared enough to do so. I had experienced a similar situation at that very chain before, but no counter rep had ever made me that offer. Be sure you know how to use your company's systems to help customers—and then be sure you actually use them.

Helping your customers to not feel hassled is incredibly important to creating Hero-Class customer experiences. The research is clear: The more effort customers have to put forth to do business with us, the more disloyal they will be. Help your customers enjoy easy, hassle-free experiences, and you'll find that they stick around longer and complain less.

Notes

1. Matthew Dixon, Nick Toman, and Rick Delisi, "It Doesn't Pay to Delight a Customer," CEB, http://www.executiveboard.com/exbd/sales-service/effortless-experience/about/index.page?. Accessed September 23, 2014.

CHAPTER 19

Service Trigger #4: Being Faced with Incompetence

Is there anything more frustrating than having a service issue and dealing with someone who simply does not know what he is doing? When you come face-to-face with incompetence, it stinks. Now, incompetence is a harsh word, but if you're on the front lines of customer interaction, it's a word you will hear. So I want to be clear what we are talking about when we discuss incompetence. What we're really talking about is the customer's *perception* of competence, and that perception is highly informed by customers' expectations—realistic or not.

For example, a customer at a bank might be upset that the first person she speaks to cannot help her with an issue. The customer could consider that person incompetent, even though the agent, due to security protocols, simply does not have the access to the information needed to resolve the customer's issue. It's unfair, but that is how the customer might interpret the situation.

Of course, customers don't always misperceive incompetence. Sometimes a service rep doesn't know how to solve an issue or is unclear if she has the necessary authority. Sometimes she is new to the job, and the more experienced person she was shadowing is at lunch. Furthermore, customers not only react to perceived individual incompetence but to perceived organizational incompetence. Incompetence magnifies mistakes. So if a customer has dealt with an incompetent person in your organization, future mistakes may be magnified, even if the customer is dealing with your organization's A-Team. And future mistakes, no matter who makes them, will feed what the customer sees as a pattern and reinforce her view of an organization that can't get its act together.

As you can see, the topic of incompetence has many layers, and the word does not necessarily suggest a judgment of the service professional's abilities or skills. Even when a service rep lacks the skills needed to perform a specific task, it doesn't mean he is not a competent professional overall or a competent person in general. It simply means he has a hole in his game that needs to be filled.

So if the perception of competence is so deeply in the mind of the beholder, how do you on the front lines work to make sure you don't pull the incompetence trigger?

- **Be the best you can be.** *"Are there areas where I struggle in my job?" "Are there certain functions where I feel less than comfortable?" "Are there times when I have frustrated customers because I didn't have the skills, knowledge, or authority to resolve the issue?"* If you answered yes to some of these questions, don't feel bad. Every frontline service rep can probably answer yes to each one. No training program is ever complete, and no training manual can ever cover every possible situation that might arise.

  Identify the areas where you feel uncomfortable and ask your manager for more training in that area. Do not feel pressure. Depending on the situation, the "training" might be as simple as a conversation. *"I had a customer who wanted to use a traveler's check; how should I handle that in the future?"*

  Observe more experienced reps. If you have some highly skilled members on your team, watch how they handle situations you don't feel comfortable with yet. Observe them and talk to them. Most people are flattered if you ask for advice. If you're in an environment where you compete for commission sales, you might find some who are unwilling to help, but in most cases, people are happy to share their knowledge to improve the team. The better you are, the easier their jobs are.

- **Get customers to the right place.** If you're not the one solving the issue, then make sure you know right department or people to pass the customer to in order to get it resolved quickly. In Chapter 20, we'll discuss how to avoid shuffling customers around. One of the primary ways to do this—and to make you, the next service rep in line, and your entire organization seem competent—is to get the customer to the right department or person the first time.

- **Reframe the customer's perspective.** While everything a customer feels is a matter of perspective, competence seems to be particularly subjective. Therefore, helping to reframe the customer's perspective can be an effective way to help reset expectations and perceptions of competence. We'll discuss framing in much more detail in Chapter 63; for now, here are two quick tips:

  1. If you're new on the job, let the customer know it. One of the times every service rep is not fully competent is when first starting in a position. Fortunately, most customers are understanding. If you are new, don't be afraid to admit it; customers will often cut you some slack. Remember, you should tell a customer you're new to help provide her with a better context for what's happening, not to provide an excuse for it. If you thank them for their patience and don't come across as if you are making excuses, most customers will be fairly forgiving.

  2. Let the customer know that the issue she is experiencing is not your organization's usual delivery of service. Simply telling a customer, *"This is not how we usually perform,"* can help shift her view of you and your company from one of incompetence to one of having made a mistake. People are more tolerant of mistakes because they know a mistake doesn't necessarily need to happen again. On the other hand, a perception of incompetence is much more damaging because it affects what the customer thinks of your organization overall and creates the perception that he can expect similar issues going forward.

Being faced with incompetence, perceived or actual, is maddening for most customers. Do your best to make sure your skills are well rounded and that you know how to properly direct customers when you cannot resolve an issue. Of course, the more issues you can solve yourself the better, because if there is one thing almost every customer hates, it's being shuffled.

CHAPTER 20

Service Trigger #5: Being Shuffled

It happens thousands of times a day, perhaps tens of thousands. A customer calls a retail store's 800 number with a problem. He is confronted with a nice service rep who speaks with him for a few minutes. The rep asks questions, takes down information, and then tells the customer, "Please hold on while I connect you to the Claims Department; they should be able to help you."

Of course, we all know what happens when the customer gets to Claims: He has to repeat the information. The rep in Claims is pleasant and eager to help, but after the customer has repeated his entire story, it turns out that the customer is a Diamond Club member. The customer needs to call the Diamond Club 800 number instead of the standard 800 number.

The customer, now beyond frustrated, calls the Diamond Club 800 number, where a very nice rep says, "My pleasure, sir. If you could just describe the problem for me, I'll make sure I can connect you with someone who can address your issue." The service rep then wonders why the customer explodes at her.

Being shuffled is an immediate trigger for most people. In most industries, the term used to describe passing customers to another department or rep is *transfer*. Every time you transfer a customer, you are automatically creating a negative experience. One research study by the customer experience analytics firm ClickFox presented customers with a list of service interactions and asked them which ones frustrated them most. Forty-one percent of respondents said "having to speak with multiple agents and starting over every time" was the most frustrating.[1] Being shuffled truly is a sensitive trigger for many people.

Accordingly, one of the best ways to consistently deliver great customer experiences is to minimize the number of transfers. This begins with management creating systems and procedures that help reduce the reasons customers are transferred. On the service floor, reps can effectively use these systems by proactively taking the opportunity to help customers get their issues resolved without a transfer and by making the transfers that are necessary as painless as possible. By employing the following ideas, you can help to not just minimize transfers but to make them more effective:

- **Know your colleagues and infrastructure.** Obviously, you will not be able to change major systems or security protocols in your organization (though you can try to provide constructive feedback to management about the obstacles that stand between you and delivering a great customer experience). However, you'll be surprised by the many ways you have the power to minimize transfers.

  For instance, let's say you work at a large hardware store. Could you and your team put together an informal list of areas in which staff members have special knowledge? Perhaps Jim has a lawnmower repair business on the side. He's your go-to guy for lawnmower questions. Perhaps Pam used to work at a nursery. She's your go-to gal for lawn and garden questions.

  In addition to knowing the capabilities of your colleagues, it's important to understand the powers inherent in your operational infrastructure. You want to know who in your organization is empowered to do what. Try to understand what keyholders, department heads, or assistant managers are empowered to do. Every manager has had a service rep say something like, "Oh, I thought only you were allowed to handle those." Think about it. You don't want to put a customer issue on your manager's desk for Monday when a keyholder can solve the issue on the spot.

- **Prepare the customer for the transfer.** Is there anything more frustrating than telling your long story to a customer service rep only to be told at the end of it that you will need to talk to someone else? You can avoid this dynamic by letting the customer know as quickly as possible that you will not be the one to assist him with his final resolution. Admittedly, this is not always easy. (See Chapter 62 for specific techniques to address this challenge.)

Once you've let the customer know you will have to transfer him, try your best to set expectations about when, where, and how his issue will be resolved. This is a sensitive subject because—let's just get it out in the open—some reps will avoid having this conversation. They know the customer is not going to be happy with the process, and it's easier to pass someone along and let the blowup occur after the transfer. Don't be that person. You might have to deal with a little more drama if you have the conversation, but in most cases, the customer's reaction to having the process described will be less severe than it would be to being surprised later in the process.

- **Prep the next rep**. Whenever possible you want to prepare the rep receiving the customer for the transfer. Let the rep know the customer's name, the issue, and any other data that might be relevant to the person taking over the issue. When possible, connect the customer to the next rep personally and facilitate the handoff. In the customer service industry, this is called a *warm transfer*. The key takeaway is to make sure you prepare the next rep to help the customer as effectively as possible.

Being shuffled is one of the most frustrating parts of being a customer, and it's a strong trigger for many people. Yet transfers are inevitable. The customer will not always end up in the right place with the right person with the right answer. Work with your management and teammates to find ways to proactively minimize transfers or to make them as effective as possible. When transfers are necessary, just be aware of how frustrating even one transfer is for the customer and use the techniques above to make them as painless as you can.

Notes

1. ClickFox, *Customer Tipping Point Survey Results,* http://web.click fox.com/rs/clickfox/images/cf-survey-results-customer-tipping-point-2010vs2011.pdf. Downloaded September 23, 2014.

CHAPTER 21

Service Trigger #6: Being Powerless

Despite what you read these days about empowered consumers and the power of social media, it's my contention that customers feel more powerless now than ever before. In fact, much of the voice of the customer being expressed through social media is *because* people feel so powerless in their relationships with organizations.

Let's face it: Companies have gotten larger and in many cases less personal. By 2013, the five largest banks in the United States held 44 percent of the banking assets, compared to 23 percent in the year 2000. That means the top five banks almost doubled their share of the entire domestic banking market in a little less than a decade and a half.[1] Similarly, as of 2013, four mobile-phone carriers accounted for 93 percent of the market, up from 61 percent in 2003.[2] From airlines to broadband Internet, consumers are increasingly dealing with megacorporations in many aspects of their lives. While big does not necessarily mean bad—some large corporations deliver excellent customer service—the aggregate impact of this trend is that consumers are faced with fewer choices and more impersonal customer relationships.

Take common monopolies like the government or utility companies. Who among us has not had an experience with a government agency or a utility when we have felt completely frustrated, powerless, and like we were at the mercy of uncaring, unfeeling employees who seemingly had never been coached or trained in customer service in their entire lives? Nowadays, that feeling is being experienced more regularly by customers in an increasing number of industries.

Only a few generations ago, customers would walk down to the corner market or the small-town bank and have a personal conversation with the owners when they had an issue. Sure, it was not all wine and roses—some small-town bankers had monopolies, some corner storeowners were jerks—but overall, customers *felt* more powerful. Not anymore.

As I mentioned in Chapter 14, most of the Seven Service Triggers arise out of an accumulation of experiences, and one experience that is common to most consumers in the United States is that their interactions as customers are increasingly becoming dominated by a lack of personal relationship with the companies they do business with. This does not mean all large companies are this way, but it does mean customers are more sensitive than ever to feeling powerless and to the companies and frontline professionals who make them feel that way.

In the previous chapters in this part, we have discussed specific techniques for addressing a particular trigger. This trigger is different. The antidote to customers' feeling powerless is more about an attitude than about any specific technique. It's about being aware that customers feel this way and giving them high levels of communication and attention so they know they have a hero in the organization who is working for them. The easiest way to prevent the powerless trigger from being pulled is to make sure that your customer knows he is not alone and that he never feels like just another number.

Notes

1. Hester Peirce and Robert Greene, "The Decline of US Small Banks (2000–2013)," Mercatus Center, George Washington University, February 24, 2014, http://mercatus.org/publication/decline-us-smallbanks -2000-2013. Accessed September 23, 2014.

2. Jon Metzler, "6 Years After the iPhone Launched, Just 4 Big Carriers Are Left Standing," VentureBeat, July 8, 2013, http://venturebeat .com/2013/07/08/iphone-carrier-consolidation/. Accessed September 23, 2014.

CHAPTER 22

Service Trigger #7: Being Disrespected

Respect. It could be one of the most important and at the same time one of the most meaningless words in the English language. Obviously, the concept of respect is extremely important to customer service. If a customer feels disrespected by you or someone in your organization, almost nothing you do will matter until her feelings about being disrespected are addressed. Yet despite the importance of the concept of respect, the word borders on having no meaning at all. We know what it means generally, but each person's concept of respect is so individual and varies so wildly from the next person's that it makes it virtually impossible to nail down a firm framework for respecting customers.

Despite this challenge, we have to talk about being disrespected as a service trigger, because the impact of that trigger being pulled can be disastrous, both for a company's relationship with that customer and for your interaction with that customer. The individual nature of disrespect makes it particularly challenging to preempt— you never really know what someone will take as disrespectful—so the easiest way to prevent the disrespect trigger from being pulled is to play the odds: Do the things that are likely to make most people feel respected. In general, that means using the core customer service ideas we'll discuss throughout the rest of this book, including obvious actions like smiling, making eye contact, and saying "Thank you." In customer service, the basics of courtesy and professionalism are the building blocks of respect.

Obviously, you'll never get it right 100 percent of the time, so you need to know what to do when someone feels disrespected. Our customers often let us know when they feel they've been disrespected. Sometimes they say outright, "You've disrespected me," or the like. Other times they use code words or phrases, such as, "Your rep was rude," or, "Your organization doesn't care about me," or "Why would you put me through this?" These examples demonstrate different ways a customer might tell you she feels disrespected by you, your team, or your organization.

Once a customer feels disrespected and you start to pick up those signals, it's important to respond with language that shows respect. One quick tip is to make sure to incorporate the word "respect" itself into your conversation: *"I apologize for how my colleague made you feel. I know he has tremendous respect for customers and would never intentionally be disrespectful."* Also, be sure to use other key words such as *value, appreciate,* and *important* when you sense a customer feels disrespected: *"We value your business, and you are important to us even if we didn't show that in this situation. I'm here to make sure you understand how much we appreciate your business."*

As we examine communication skills and handling difficult situations in subsequent parts of this book, you'll learn some extremely powerful language and techniques that can be applied when a customer feels disrespected. For now, the most important thing to remember is that proactively helping your customers to feel valued and respected is the first step toward ensuring they don't feel disrespected.

PART FOUR

BE A GREAT TEAMMATE

CHAPTER **23**

Why Teamwork Matters

You've no doubt heard someone say it before, and perhaps you've even said it yourself: "*Why should I care about the team? I come in, I do my job, and I go home. End of story.*" The good news is that if this is your philosophy, you're not alone; plenty of others feel the same way. The bad news is that if you've adopted this attitude, you will probably never be happy at work—anywhere.

Human beings are social creatures. We need other people. Unless you're living in the wild using rocks for tools, you depend on people every day. "*I don't need anyone; I take care of myself,*" I've heard people say proudly. Really, did you manufacture that car you're driving? Did you harvest those vegetables you're eating? Did you create the fabrics in the shirt you're wearing? In society, we depend on others, if only in these most basic, obvious ways.

In our organizations, we depend on others too. Whether you want to be or not, you are tied together with your coworkers. The economy provides us with an apt analogy for teamwork. The health of our economy is based on many complex factors about which there is much disagreement; yet, most economists would agree that one of the primary contributors to a healthy economy is confidence in what others will do. When business owners have confidence that consumers will buy their products, they hire more people. When those people spend their paychecks on goods and services, other companies hire more people. In any group, individuals are more likely to take positive action that benefits them all when they have confidence that other members are doing the same.

Teams at work follow a similar principle. The success of teams depends in no small part on confidence in the actions of others as well. If Sarah thinks that Jenny and John do not pull their weight, she will be more likely to not work as hard. When Maria sees Frank slacking off, she will begin to question whether she is the only employee on the service floor doing any work. Eventually, the results of this mindset will negatively impact the organization and its customers.

It's important to note that while society and our economy tie us together, they do not stop us from growing individually. In bad times and good, individuals have opportunities to achieve success. For the majority, though, it's simply easier to succeed when the economy— the group—is doing better. Similarly, being part of a team does not make someone less independent or self-sufficient; it simply means she is stronger when the team is stronger. The better the organization does, the more chances each individual in that company has for success. As the old saying goes, a rising tide lifts all boats. While the saying is not always accurate, it's a sound reminder that the better your team does, the better you can do.

So that's why teamwork matters. The better the team performs, the happier the customers are, the better the business does, and the easier and more opportunity filled your job will be. Hero-Class customer service cannot exist without teamwork, yet few frontline customer service books cover this critical subject. This is understandable, because focusing on teamwork involves discussing mindset as much as technique. It also involves facing an uncomfortable truth: The only team member whose actions you have any control over is you.

In this part of the book, we're going to discuss some ways you can be a great teammate, as well as how you can help elevate your team to be more effective and more pleasant to be a member of. Let's start by looking at one of the greatest challenges team members face: what to do when a teammate is not carrying his own weight.

CHAPTER 24

Rise Above, Don't Stoop Down

It happens to everyone. Eventually, you will work with a jerk, you will work with a slacker, and you will work with a liar. Sometimes all three of these will be the same person. Working with lousy teammates is one of the biggest discouragements to being a great teammate. These coworkers—let's not call them teammates—suck the energy out of teams and make life unpleasant on the service floor. They don't know what it's like to be part of a team; it's all about them.

When working with individuals who care only about themselves, the challenge is to make sure you don't stoop down to their level. Toxic coworkers have a gravitational pull all to themselves. They can easily suck you into their vortex. *"Jenny didn't straighten the sales table when she closed last week. Let's see how she likes a messy sales table when she opens tomorrow."* It's a natural human reaction that we've all had many times in our lives. If *you're* not pulling your weight, why should I? The problem is that it's likely Jenny will not be the only one affected by your actions. Let's see what can happen when you decide to teach Jenny a lesson:

- Jenny is not the one who has to straighten out your mess the next morning. She is assigned to the stockroom, and your friend Jim has to clean it up.
- The phone is already ringing off the hook before the doors even open, so the sales table is not cleaned until two hours after opening. The store's morning customers see a messy table and get a terrible impression of your company.
- Your manager sees the table and looks to see who closed the

night before. It was you, and it's the week before your annual evaluation and raise. Who ends up affected now?

Does it stink when a coworker is not pulling her weight? Of course it does. The reality is that in most jobs, it can take time before problem coworkers leave or are fired. This means that sometimes you have to live with slackers on your team—sometimes for a lot longer than you would want. I want to add that frontline employees are not the only people who have to deal with this challenge. This dynamic happens at every level of an organization. From the front lines to the executive board, there's often someone who is getting a free ride on the efforts of the other team members. You may as well learn how to handle it now, because it's simply a part of business.

Specific ways of handling dysfunctional teams or slacking coworkers is beyond the scope of this book. What I would like you to take away from this chapter is that a healthy team is important to your success, to your customer's experience, and to your company's health. Whenever you have a slacker on your team, ask yourself this: Is the best way to deal with that person's being a terrible team-mate to become one too? You already know the answer. Find a way to rise above the behavior of underperforming teammates and be sure to support the members of your team who are standing beside you on the front lines, giving customers great experiences and making work more pleasant. While you might feel you are being taken advantage of once in a while, most of the time being a great team-mate is its own reward.

So, let's focus on what being a great teammate looks like on the front lines of service.

CHAPTER 25

"It's Showtime"

My father, a retail manager and later wholesale distribution entre-preneur, had a number of business sayings that he used when I was growing up. One of those sayings stands out as a definitive ethic for all customer-facing professionals: It's showtime.

When it came to business, it didn't matter how my dad felt. About to collapse because he was sick, ready to fall over from lack of sleep, prepared to call it a day but with one more meeting left—it was all irrelevant. When it was showtime, he left everything else behind.

If my father wasn't at 100 percent, he would pause for a moment before walking into the meeting or picking up the phone. He would stand up straight, smile, and say, "It's showtime." (He was a professional musician in his younger years, so he often thought in show business terms.) My father knew that the hall-mark of a professional was having his best face on when doing business. His customers deserved it. His vendors deserved it. His teammates deserved it.

For customer-facing roles, the idea of showtime works on two levels—when you're in front of customers and when you're at work but not in front of customers. One of the ways the Dis-ney Corporation creates its legendary customer experiences is by viewing the experience as a show. Disney refers to its employ-ees as cast members and refers to being customer-facing as being onstage. In his book *Be Our Guest*, Theodore Kinni explains the onstage concept:

> The Disney theme parks and their many cast members make a clear distinction between being onstage and offstage.

In Disney-speak, cast members are onstage whenever they are in the public areas of the park and in front of guests. They are offstage when they are behind the scenes and out of their guests' sight.[1]

The idea of being onstage is important because it sets the expectation that when you're on the service floor or otherwise in front of customers you have your game face on. It's not about being inauthentic or not being yourself, but about acting in a manner conducive to your setting and to creating great customer experiences.

The concept of showtime also extends to when you are offstage. While your behavior might be a little more relaxed, a little more informal when you're not in front of customers, being a great team-mate means you remember you're on the job from the time you walk through the door to the time you leave. That means leaving your personal life at the door when you arrive at work. Day-care issues. Sick relatives. Bad relationships. Everyone's got drama. When you get to work, it doesn't matter. It's showtime, and you need to leave personal matters behind.

I'm not trying to be insensitive. Things happen that completely knock us over: the recent death of a parent, news of an eviction, preparation for an impending surgery, to name a few. When those rare, terrible things happen though, your managers and your team-mates will be much more understanding if you are someone who normally leaves your personal life at the door. If you have your game face on every day, your colleagues will understand how serious it is when you do not.

If you want to deliver Hero-Class customer service, propel your career forward, and be a respected team member, one of your first steps is making sure you have your professional face on when you get to work.

Just remember that when you walk through those doors, it's showtime.

Notes

1. Theodore Kinni, *Be Our Guest: Perfecting the Art of Customer Service* (Disney Editions, 2003), Kindle ed., ch. 1, sec.: "Defining Practical Magic," loc. 208.

CHAPTER 26

The Clothes Make the Rep

Whether you wear your own clothes to work or a company uniform, the appearance of your clothing makes a huge difference in how customers perceive you and your company. As we will discuss in Chapter 32, customers make snap, subconscious judgments as soon as they see you, meaning you are being judged on how you look (and how you sound). Facial expressions, hair, posture, and tattoos all impact how someone perceives you and how they judge your likability and competence. Among the biggest impacts on the impression you make is your clothing. As was once captured in the title of a 1980s business book, you have to dress for success.

Let's start with what many of you are probably thinking. Dress for success? Do you want me to wear a tuxedo to work the service floor? Of course not. In fact, overdressing for your job would be distracting and off-putting to customers. The goal is not to dress *up* but to dress *well*.

If you don't wear a uniform to work, you have more flexibility. Your goal should be to be one of the sharpest-looking people on your service floor, within reason. You don't want to overdress; you just want to be among the top few people in appearance.

If you wear a uniform to work, you obviously have less flexibility. This is good for the most part. In most cases, it's less expensive and time consuming than having to come up with different outfits. The catch is that often frontline reps tend to let their uniforms deteriorate a bit more than they do their own clothing. This is a mistake.

The key when focusing on clothing is simple. Make sure of the following:

- Clothing is clean and not wrinkled.
- Clothing fits properly.
- Clothing is not faded or worn.
- Shirts are tucked in, when appropriate.
- Shoes are clean looking and shined, when appropriate.
- Clothing and accessories match and are within industry norms.
- Jewelry is within industry norms.

Your goal is to look clean and professional. You're not trying to stand out; you're trying to instill confidence in your teammates, your managers, and your customers in your competence.

I do want to note that I understand there is a financial aspect to this topic. Clothes cost money. Nicer clothes cost even more money. However, I've known many people working frontline jobs who have managed to look very sharp with a limited budget. They were creative, mixed and matched pieces, and took care of their clothing. Obviously, your clothing should be adapted to your environment, but in general, don't worry about having the nicest styles or wearing premium brands. Simply focus on looking neat and professional. Make looking nice something that is important to you, and do the best with what you can.

No matter what your position—from insurance salesperson to department store clerk—clothes are important, and they always make the rep.

CHAPTER 27

Always Be Professional

When I've done trainings in the past, I've often asked, "What does professionalism mean to you?" The answers, as you might imagine, are as varied as the people responding. Like many vague concepts (respect, for instance), professionalism is in the eye of the beholder. Yet certain tenets seem to be common for almost everyone and every organization.

I believe each of the following characteristics is a component of professionalism:

- Being punctual
- Using appropriate language
- Executing job responsibilities as expected
- Looking professional
- Not speaking ill of customers, coworkers, or managers

Coming from a managerial perspective, I cannot overemphasize how important professionalism is to most managers and supervisors. You can be the smartest, the hardest-working, and even the most likable person on the service floor, but if you act unprofessionally, especially in front of customers, most good managers will be unable to look past it. It will overshadow whatever positive contributions you make. Acting professionally is the entrance exam you must pass to be taken seriously.

If you're reading this book, I know you're someone who cares and wants to improve. One of the most difficult challenges for managers is when employees who mean well and generally do a good job still act unprofessionally. It happens. I've seen well-meaning, highly skilled employees engage in unprofessional behavior. It's usually not due to neglect or a failure to care, but to a lack of focus and awareness. Here are a few ways I have seen unprofessional behavior that was unintentional:

- Talking inappropriately with teammates in front of customers
- Not paying immediate attention to customers
- Not respecting personal space or professional boundaries with teammates
- Oversharing personal information in the break room

People who care and who want to do a good job sometimes engage in unprofessional behavior simply because they let themselves get a little too comfortable or aren't paying attention. It can happen to anyone.

The important part is to realize what is professional and what is not. Always keep in mind the Disney concept of being onstage. It's okay to talk about your weekend at work (well, the respectable parts of your weekend), but it's not okay to do so when customers can hear you. Similarly, it's okay to complain about a belligerent customer when you get home; it's not appropriate to do so in the break room. Okay, okay, I'm a realist—you're going to talk about it. But have a filter, and a level that you don't go past.

In the end, professionalism is about self-discipline and self-control. You know what being a professional looks like. If you want to be known and treated as one, you simply have to live up to your own idea of professionalism when at work—even if it means holding your tongue once in a while.

CHAPTER 28

Set the Next Shift Up for Success

In many frontline positions, you'll have members of your team who have the same job you do, whose lives you directly impact, and who you often never see. These are the teammates who work different shifts. No matter how the shifts are organized at your job, one of the most important things you can do to be a great teammate is to set the next shift up for success. Whether you're opening the store and making sure things are straight for those who close up at night or you're working weekday shifts and setting the stage for the weekend crew, you can make sure team members on the shifts that follow are ready to roll by taking the time to proactively address potential issues.

Preparing the next shift for success comes down to making sure you have prepared the service floor adequately and to evaluating what the next shift might need to know so it's not blindsided. In addition to the basic checklist processes your company likely has for closing out certain shifts, here are a few specific questions you can ask yourself to help set the next shift up to win:

- **What issues can you anticipate and preempt for the next shift?** Perhaps you've discovered that the language on the new sales sign is unclear to customers and is causing a lot of service issues. You should discuss changing or removing the sign with your manager before the rush hits the evening shift.

- **Were there customer issues that were not resolved on your shift?** For instance, a customer had an issue with a return the night before. The note said the customer would be in meetings until after 3:00 p.m., so the morning shift can't call him to resolve the issue. The afternoon shift will need to be made aware so it can address the situation.

- **What operational issues arose on your shift that haven't been addressed?** Did you run out of glass cleaner and were unable to clean the display cases? Let the next shift know it was not on purpose and that someone will need to make a run to the store while business is still slow. Is the scanner on register 18 broken? Let the next shift know, so no one opens his drawer and finds out about the broken scanner while trying to check out his first customer.

Of course, what needs to happen on each shift and what's expected of each team member on each shift is specific to each organization and each manager. You'll likely have a defined set of responsibilities and procedures for whatever shift you work. But wherever you work, once your checklist is done, you can take it a step further and ask yourself questions like the ones above. If you take a few moments to proactively think about the potential problems the next shift might encounter (and if your colleagues on other shifts do the same), you and your teammates will find that every shift is a bit easier to handle.

CHAPTER 29

Five Reasons Customer Documentation Matters

Do you want to know one of the essential signs that a company has a Hero-Class customer service culture? Customer documentation. Yes, I said *documentation*.

Now let's just get this out in the open from the start: Documentation is boring, and there's nothing I can say to make it more exciting. What I can do, however, is tell you how important good documentation is and how crucial it is to being a great teammate, making your customers' lives less complicated, and making your job easier.

Documentation is one of the secret ingredients of a customer-centric organization, and it's one that few people talk about. If I speak with an owner or manager and want to know how serious she is about creating a customer-centric culture, one area I will ask about is the business's system of customer documentation. Why? Because good documentation makes Hero-Class customer service possible!

When I refer to documentation, I am really referring to two things: either actual documents that are part of the record—a purchase order or liability waiver, for instance—or the recording of events or interactions. For our purposes here, documentation refers to things like recording the conversation you had in the hallway about room service, the fact that the customer's room was not ready upon arrival, and the emails the customer sent before his stay requesting extra towels. I view documentation as recording information for the sake of future experiences, even when the documentation is not necessary to the current experience. Customer documentation is recording what *should* be recorded, not just what *has* to be recorded.

For customers, good documentation can mean the difference between an easily resolved service issue and one that takes far longer than necessary. For you and your fellow teammates, good customer documentation can mean the difference between adequate preparation and being caught completely unawares. Let's take a hypothetical scenario and see how documentation can improve your customers' lives and your own.

Let's say you have a customer who brought in an item for repair. She has been waiting over a week and is exceptionally angry. Unfortunately, you are waiting for the part to arrive from the supplier, and you have already missed one promised date to the customer. To add to the fun, the customer wants to be contacted by phone only. How can good documentation help this situation be addressed more effectively?

- **A customer's past experience is often essential to her future experience.** Because your teammates recorded the customer's previous interactions, you know this is the second time she has had a delayed repair. This helps you understand that the customer is particularly sensitive about this issue and suggests that you need to be *extra* proactive in your communication with the customer.
- **Information shared is information made useful.** On the night shift, you get an email saying the part is in stock and will arrive at your store Tuesday. This information is useless unless you share it with those who can address it with the customer the next day. At minimum, the information needs to be entered in the customer's record so it can be found by your teammates on future shifts. Even better, you should let those on the morning shift know about the update and encourage them to reach out to the customer proactively.
- **Knowing a customer's history is great service in and of itself.** As you know from Service Trigger #5, Being Shuffled, it's one of the greatest annoyances in all of customer service when customers have to repeat their story and details repeatedly to

different people in the organization. Recording that history so the next team member can use it improves the customer experience automatically.

- **It's helpful to know the facts.** One of the challenges with this customer is that she says no one from your organization ever calls to update her. Because the team members recorded the times that messages were left for her, you know that this is not true. You may or may not use this information with the customer (see Chapter 60 for more on this topic), but it is important to know that you do not have a problem in-house.

Clearly, documentation contributes significant value to your team and its ability to serve its customers. At the same time, too much documentation can be as detrimental as too little, so it's important to use discretion when documenting customer interactions or situations. Everyone in business today is confronted with information overload, and the most typical response is simply to ignore any information that does not represent a flaming emergency. Documenting everything can be the equivalent of documenting nothing.

While customer documentation is neither exciting nor inspirational, embracing its importance will go a long way toward helping you and your teammates deliver Hero-Class customer service. Before we leave this very exciting subject (we're almost done, I promise), let's take a quick look at how to document effectively.

CHAPTER **30**

Document Quickly and Effectively

While approaches to effective documentation vary widely across organizations and circumstances, the one principle that applies almost universally is: Record it or lose it.

If you work in a customer-facing role, chances are you probably have a lot going on. And in most cases, if you don't document the information from a customer interaction during or immediately afterward, one of three things will happen:

- Your notes will not get recorded.
- Your notes will be recorded but will be missing crucial details.
- Your notes will have errors in them.

Communication is tough enough to document accurately when you record the notes in real time. For instance, were you able to accurately record what the customer was trying to say? Did you understand what the customer was really most upset about? It's even tougher to get the details right when you've waited four hours and spoken with 23 other customers since then.

Let's face it, you can't write thorough notes when you have a line of customers in front of you or a stacked set of calls on hold waiting for your attention. If you don't have time for full documentation, try to take a few moments to create "holder notes," either digitally or on paper, that get the heart of the matter. Here's an example:

> Jillian Smith
> 3:55p 08/12/14
> Upset about delivery. Piece late and broken.
> Too large for her to rebox for return.
> Called 3 times. No response. Came in very upset.
> Wants delivery people to box item & take away.
> Contact 407-555-5555

This note should take about 45 seconds to write, and it will give you something to jog your memory. If you have a customer staring at you, perhaps you write less and just get the bare facts down in 15 seconds:

> Jillian Smith 3:55 08/12
> Piece late and broken. Too big to rebox.
> Called 3x. Wants us to box & take away.
> 407-555-5555

This should be enough information that if you return to the issue within a few hours, you will likely remember the details. Holder notes are a temporary measure when you cannot document in the moment.

What constitutes effective documentation is so context sensitive that it's virtually impossible to offer specific guidance. In the following list, you'll find a few basic principles for effective documentation that should apply to most organizations:

- Include the four Ws of the situation: who, what, when, and where.
- Note the time, date, and, if not obvious, location of your interaction with the customer.
- When appropriate, record the names of anyone, especially within the company, who was a witness to the situation.
- Use direct quotes to document something the customer said, particularly when they involve disputed facts or inappropri-

ate comments. This makes it clear that you are not the one saying it. For example:

> Customer said "the frame arrived in seven pieces." Customer was very upset. She said I was "a lying piece of ___" and that our whole company is "full of thieving scumbags."

Depending on your company, you can spell out the foul language (I'm not doing so in the book). Personally, I recommend writing out the actual words so they will be part of the record, but be sure of your company's policy or approach.

- Document what you know could be relevant in the future to you or to another department. The more experience you have at your company, the better you will be at this. You will learn that the purchasing department is going to need the invoice number and that you'd better include it. You will learn that recording a customer's complaint about not receiving bills is important because often customers use this approach to avoid payment, and documenting the pattern can make a difference.

In the big picture, good documentation is both a selfish and selfless act; it helps you and your teammates be prepared for future customer interactions. It's also an act for which there is no immediate gratification; the benefits are often in the future and may never come at all. Documentation always has value though, because knowing a customer's history is important to providing excellent proactive service. You just have to realize that documentation is about documenting *most* situations, knowing that only *a few* of those situations will arise again.

CHAPTER 31

When to Help a Teammate with a Customer

One of my employees once asked me, "How do I know when to jump in and help someone with a customer?" It was not a question I had thought much about. While I had discussed this scenario in training, I had not given much consideration to the level of uncertainty that team members can have in these situations. This was an area where I was disconnected from the front lines.

As a business owner, I can easily jump into a conversation with a customer. In fact, if you're the owner or manager, you are generally welcomed into any customer conversation as someone in authority who can "do more" to help resolve the customer's issue. But the question my employee asked made me consider what an associate should do when she is not the boss or manager. What if this individual holds the same position as the one assisting the customer? How should frontline professionals handle these situations?

While there are no hard and fast rules for situations like this, below you'll find four scenarios to help you evaluate when to jump in and help a teammate who is working with a customer:

1. The teammate is giving inaccurate information. If you hear a teammate giving a customer inaccurate information, that's usually a strong signal to involve yourself in the conversation, particularly if that information could come back to haunt the customer and the company later. In customer service, when a team member leaves a customer with false expectations, she is creating problems for teammates down the line.

2. The teammate is no longer focused on a solution. When you see that your teammate is being reactive and is more focused on defending himself than on satisfying the customer, then it's time to get involved. If you step in gently and focus on solutions, your teammate will hopefully be inspired to rejoin you on a productive path.

3. The customer is not responding well to your teammate. When it's obvious the customer is reacting to your teammate as much as to the situation or the company, a fresh face can help change the direction of the conversation.

4. The customer wants someone with more authority. Even if you do not technically have more formal authority, you can occasionally adopt an air of authority by conveying knowledge or experience. *"No sir, I'm not a manager, but I've been with the company for three years, and I'm very familiar with the product you're talking about."* This move implicitly knocks your teammate a bit—it's the same as saying I have more knowledge than the person you've been talking to—so it should be used with care and only when a situation is really in a downward spiral. We will discuss using your authority with customers further in Chapter 65.

Stepping in to help a teammate is an inherently delicate business. You need to be aware of your relationship with the teammate and of his general disposition. Egos are fragile things, and stepping in to save a situation can inherently be seen by less secure teammates as insulting or patronizing. If the goal is to help the customer, you can only achieve it if your actions do not make the situation worse.

The four scenarios above will give you some fairly solid guidelines on when to consider stepping in to help a teammate, but each specific instance will be dictated by who is in the situation as much as what the situation is.

CHAPTER **32**

Make That First Impression Count

The field of psychology is filled with research studies probing the incredible speed at which our minds form judgments about people and about the impact these judgments can have.

On the front lines, understanding the importance of first impressions is essential to knowing how to start off customer interactions on the right foot. Customers are making up their minds about you and your organization in the briefest of moments, and these early impressions have a direct impact on their subsequent service experience. How fast do people form impressions of others? One study shows it can be in as little as a tenth of a second.[1] Whether these impressions are fair or accurate is irrelevant, because they are happening regardless. As a customer-facing professional, it's in your best interest to shape these initial moments to your advantage as much as possible.

I like to break down the characteristics of first impressions into two basic categories: environmental and interactional. Environmental characteristics are the things the customer observes as she walks through the door. Are the windows dirty? Is the counter messy? Are the reps dressed unprofessionally? When a customer enters your store, she is analyzing all these things—even if she doesn't know she's doing it. As discussed in Chapter 26, customers are judging you based on the professionalism of your clothes and appearance. They're also judging you on your service floor.

Interactional characteristics are the details of your first exchanges with the customer. Did you walk across the service floor or around the counter to greet her? Did you smile and make eye contact? Did you seem genuinely helpful or like someone who was just going through the motions because it was your job? One study from the automotive sales industry shows that first impressions of a salesperson affect purchasing decisions.[2] Everything about you—your posture, your tone of voice, and your actions—is being evaluated by the customer in those first moments, and the impression the customer forms will either enrich or detract from your ability to provide a Hero-Class customer experience.

Fortunately, all is not lost if you make a bad first impression, though it makes your job more difficult. When training frontline staff on greeting customers and first impressions, I like to use the analogy of driving into a ditch. Imagine you're about to begin a journey, and at the very start of that journey you drive straight into a ditch. You're not going to make any progress until you get yourself out, and once you're stuck in that ditch, all your time and energy goes to getting out of it. When you make a bad first impression, you're beginning your customer interaction already in a ditch, and it becomes a lot harder to move the experience forward.

Obviously, you don't want to begin a customer interaction this way, so let's look at a few ways you can make a great first impression with a customer:

- Smile.
- Give a genuine, friendly greeting.
- Make a gesture of attentiveness, like standing up.
- Approach the customer.
- Give the customer your undivided attention.

What I love about first impressions is that they are an opportunity to set the tone for the rest of the experience. This can even be true if the customer has a history with your brand. Despite all we've discussed about customers not coming to us as blank slates and about their being preconditioned to react to service triggers, when a customer comes to *your* location for the first time or interacts with *you* for the first time, you have an opportunity. When a customer has a disposition toward a business, either positive or negative, he will often still give you, the individual, a fair shot. Unless he comes in with a huge chip already on his shoulder, you have a chance to make him feel good about your store or, at the least, about you personally.

Think about your own experiences as a customer and I'm sure you can relate. Surely you like particular locations within a chain or franchise more than others or like certain service professionals at a location even though you're not a huge fan of the business. "*I love Restaurant X, but the one on Fifth Avenue always gets my order wrong. Coffee Chain Y generally stinks, but Lisa at the Main Street location is so awesome, I keep going back.*" No matter how a customer feels walking onto your service floor for the first time, what she experiences in those first moments will be viewed through the lens that already exists. If she has a positive outlook on your brand, then you'll need to meet or exceed that expectation to set her experience on the right path. If she has a negative outlook, then you'll have to prove her expectations wrong and convince her that your location and you are different. Either way, the first impression you make will go a long way toward making or breaking that customer's experience.

Writers are counseled to avoid clichés whenever possible. Yet often a cliché exists because someone said something really well in the first place. As it happens, the old saying "You never get a second chance to make a first impression" sums up the lesson of this chapter perfectly. When a customer walks into your world for the first time, seize the opportunity to start the relationship off well by making sure you create a great first impression. You only get one shot at it, and the payoff is well worth the effort.

Notes

1. Eric Wargo, "How Many Seconds to a First Impression?" *Observer* 19, no. 7 (July 2006), Association for Psychological Science, http://www .psychologicalscience.org/index.php/publications/observer/2006/july-06/how-many-seconds-to-a-first-impression.html. Accessed September 23, 2014.

2. Joshua James Probst, "How a Customer's First Impression Impacts Sales Effectiveness in an Automotive Retail Facility with Correlation to the Purchasing Decision" (master's research paper, University of Wisconsin-Stout, 2004), http://www2.uwstout.edu/content/lib/thesis/2003/2003probstj.pdf. Accessed August 24, 2014.

CHAPTER 33

How Are You Today?

We previously discussed the idea of showtime—leaving our personal lives at the door and putting our best foot forward for customers and colleagues. Now let's look at one of the unintentional, almost habitual ways customer-facing professionals allow their personal states of mind to slip into exchanges with customers on the service floor. It happens when service reps respond to the question, *"How are you today?"*

When you ask customers how they are doing, they'll almost always ask you the same in return. All too often, the answers that service reps give contain more information than the customer needs to know. Here are some typical answers that service providers give when they are asked how they are doing: *"Fine." "Okay." "All right." "Good." "Hangin' in there." "I've been better." "No complaints."* These responses may accurately reflect how the individual feels at the moment, but none of them are positive or powerful. They call attention to the fact that something is not well, and, more important, they make the exchange about you and not about the customer. To quote Vince Vaughn's character in the movie *Wedding Crashers*, "It draws attention in a negative way."[1]

What should you say instead? How about using words like, *"Great," "Wonderful," "Excellent," "Outstanding"*? If you want to have some fun with it, you can even say something like *"Fantabulous"* or use personal finance expert Dave Ramsey's signature line: *"Better than I deserve."* Regardless of what phrase you choose, the objective is to say something that adds energy and positivity to the conversation. What good is a great smile and a warm greeting when they're followed by a halfhearted phrase like, "I'm okay"?

"But what if I'm not doing great?" I've been asked. "Isn't it dishonest to say I am?" No, I don't believe it is, and for one simple reason: No one is asking you a question they expect a real answer to. When you are greeting a customer on the service floor or passing a coworker in the hall, I hate to break it to you, but most of the time they really aren't that interested in how you're doing. They're not expecting you to stop and tell them that your kid just won the spelling bee, that your boyfriend wrecked his motorcycle, or that Aunt Beatrice just passed away. You're engaged in a superficial exchange of pleasantries. It only has meaning if you give some halfhearted answer that calls attention to yourself.

I remember a few years ago being up all night with my dying dog of 12 years, then having her pass away in my arms the next morning as the vet put her down. I had to return a call from one of my employees later that day, and when she asked how I was doing, my answer was, "Excellent." It wasn't true, but it didn't matter. If a close friend had asked the question, I would have probably told him that we had just put our dog to sleep and would have accepted some sympathy. But my employee didn't need to hear it. She needed my help with a problem, not to have her day interrupted with my personal issues. A customer would want to hear it even less.

An additional benefit to changing your approach in this area is that by altering the basic language you use to answer this question, you can actually impact how you think and feel. You might be surprised to find that when you regularly start replying to *"How are you?"* with *"Excellent,"* you will start to actually feel that way.

So choose a few words you feel comfortable with and make those your default answers; you and your customers will have a better day.

Notes

1. *Wedding Crashers* Trivia, Internet Movie Database, http://www.imdb .com/title/tt0396269/trivia. Accessed October 27, 2014.

CHAPTER 34

How to Handle
"I'm Just Browsing"

One of the most important skills you can learn as a frontline professional is when and how to respect boundaries set by a customer. In retail environments, this boundary is often created by some version of the browsing response. When you approach a customer to greet and assist, you will sometimes hear something similar to one of the following: *"I'm just browsing." "I'm just looking." "I'm just killing time."* Generally, when you're confronted with the browsing response, it means one of three things:

1. The customer really is just browsing.
2. The customer doesn't want to deal with anyone and wants to figure it out on his own.
3. The customer does not want to be "sold" and prefers to browse unassisted.

How do you know which one describes the customer in front of you? In your first contact with the customer, it doesn't actually matter. In that interaction, you should respect the browse. No matter the reason, the customer is obviously not ready to engage with anyone. That is all that matters. Whenever you receive the browsing response, your response should generally be the same: your name plus a helpful fact that opens the door for the customer to approach you later (unless using the Name Delay, as discussed in Chapter 37):

- *"That's great. My name is Adam. I'll be right over there if you need anything."*
- *"I understand. My name is Adam, in case you need any-*

thing. I'll check back in with you in a little bit to see if you have any questions."

- *"Looking around is my favorite part of shopping. I'm Adam, if you need anything. Just to let you know, we just received these new inventory scanners, and I can look up anything in the store for you right on this device."*

Also, when a customer tells you he is just browsing, there are some common responses you should avoid: *"No worries." "No problem." "That's okay."* Why is this language bad? Because the customer is entitled to browse. You don't want your language to indicate that the customer's decision to browse is not imposing on you (they don't care) or that you're giving permission for them to browse (they didn't ask you for it). Simply stick with giving your name and a helpful fact.

Now, if you've received the browsing response from a customer, you'll have a decision to make about when to reengage. This decision depends a lot on your ability to read body language and on how long the customer has been walking around. After a certain amount of time, most browsers expect someone to follow up. There's no hard-and-fast rule here. You have to make a judgment call based on the customer's demeanor and the typical patterns on your service floor. When you reengage, you want to avoid a pushy, sales approach. Generally, you should just start with some sort of checking-in line like, "I just wanted to see how you are doing." Then, you can use phrases along the lines of:

- *"Were you shopping for someone in particular?"*
- *"Were you looking for something for yourself or someone else?"*
- *"I noticed you've been looking at pants. Are you interested in the new spring items that just came in?"*

Don't push specials or deals unless you can tie them to something about which the customer has already shown interest or unless you can engage him in a conversation that naturally leads in that direction. Also, since you've already given your name in the initial interaction, try to get the customer's name so you can use it. *"By the way, I didn't catch your name earlier."* We'll discuss the importance of names in Chapter 37.

The essence of handling the browsing response is finding the sweet spot between ignoring the customer and pressuring the customer. You want to respect the browse, but you also want to remember that "I'm just browsing" should not be taken as a "No" but more as a "Not right now." The key is making sure your customer knows you're available to her without giving her the sense that you're hovering over her or pressuring her. As you'll see in Chapter 35, too much attention paid to a customer can be almost as bad as too little.

Don't Be a Helicopter Rep

In the past decade or so, the term *helicopter parent* became popular as a description of a parent who constantly hovers over his or her children, overprotecting them and microparenting. Similarly, a helicopter rep is a customer-facing professional who hovers over the customer, creating a sense of pressure and overbearing attention.

Often, helicopter reps mean to do the right thing; they are trying to be available for the customer and attempting to let the customer know she is not being ignored. It's just too much of a good thing. People need space. Even people who generally look forward to contact from frontline reps can quickly grow irritated when a service rep hovers over them or checks with them too frequently. It's like having a friend who calls to check on you every hour when you're sick. The repeated gestures are really nice, but at some point you just want to lie on the couch and binge watch *The Walking Dead*.

To add another layer of complexity, some customers don't even want minimal contact; they simply want to be left alone. On the Customers That Stick blog, I once wrote a post about self-service in retail. I was surprised to read in the comment section just how much people enjoy self-checkout. Recent data supports this. An MSNBC .com survey found that 35 percent of consumers said they "loved self-checkout lanes,"[1] and a study from the United Kingdom found that 57 percent of consumers "like self-service checkouts because it speeds up the process."[2] Regardless of whether self-service is a good thing or not (some people hate it), the takeaway from the research is that probably a third or more of your customers want to be left alone or, at most, want the minimum interaction needed to complete the transaction. When customers feel this way, it's easy to make them feel smothered.

Despite these statistics, you don't want to be inattentive or to assume that customers don't want assistance. As we discussed in the Chapter 34, you always want to make initial contact with the customer. Once you've initiated contact, however, it's important to remember that the customer may simply want to be left alone to shop and get out as fast as possible.

How do you know what the customer in front of you wants? If you're lucky, she will tell you outright: *"Can you help me find the baby strollers?"* If not, you want to pay close attention to the language the customer uses and the body language she displays. In Zen-speak, you want to be present without pressuring and to be available without attaching.

Knowing how to find the balance between attentiveness and space is one of the hallmarks of great customer service. By being aware that all customers do not want the same amount of attention and by paying close attention to the signals the customer sends you, you can avoid crossing the line from Hero-Class rep to helicopter rep.

Notes

1. Anika Anand, "Welcome Valued Customer…to More Self-Checkouts," NBC News, July 22, 2011, http://www.nbcnews.com/id/43729757/ns/business-retail/t/welcome-valued-customer-more-self-checkouts/#.U_YUHVaFmFR. Accessed August 24, 2014.

2. James Halliwell, "Unexpected Item in Self-Service Till Survey: Shoppers Want More," Grocer, August 24, 2012, http://www.thegrocer.co.uk/home/topics/technology-and-supply-chain/unexpected-item-in-self-service-till-survey/231938.article. Accessed August 24, 2014.

CHAPTER 36

Can You Remember One Thing?

Whenever we can personalize a customer experience, we've gone a long way toward making it memorable. Every customer wants to feel special, and personalization, even in very small ways, can help us create that feeling.

Of course, computerized customer relationship management (CRM) systems are the most popular way to personalize these experiences nowadays. Software today can hold a virtually limitless amount of information about customers, which is why Big Data (the large amounts of data collected from customers via their digital interactions) and mass customization are among the most talked about topics in the customer-focused fields. However, CRM systems are only as powerful as their ability to be present in the moment with a customer, and therein lies the gulf between the present and the future.

In the somewhat creepy Big Data/wearable computing future, store owners and frontline reps will likely know large amounts of information about their customers the moment they walk in the door. Either a tag in the customer's clothing or the customer's mobile phone will immediately be detected by the store, the customer's information will appear on the store computer or the rep's mobile device, and frontline reps will have access to customer information in the first moments of an interaction. Yet, for the vast majority of frontline situations, that scenario is still far in the future.

So how do you, working the service floor with little to no detailed customer data and a constantly changing customer base, personalize your customer's journey now? How do you personalize it when you're in the aisle at the home improvement store, in the deli department at the grocery store, or inside your sister's dress boutique? What do you do when the customer is a stranger?

There are a host of techniques for personalizing customer experiences, but the best quick-and-dirty trick I know is this one: Remember one thing. When you approach customers in the store, your goal is to engage them in a conversation that helps reveal their needs and wants. Your goal should be to learn as many details as you can about the customer and what that person hopes to get out of his visit. Then you should tailor your actions to deliver that experience as best you can. This level of personalization is what every service rep should strive for, and in a perfect world, it's what every frontline rep would do—every time. But let's be real—you don't always have time for all that. So when time is short, try to remember just one thing about the customer.

When speaking with the customer look for a hot spot, something that seems to be important and where you know your company can add value. Commit that one thing to memory. For example, if you had two people in the store, you could easily remember one thing about each of them: *Lady in the red dress—shopping for her daughter who is leaving for college up north. Man with the baby—looking for a birthday present for his wife who likes to "dress young."* When you check back with these customers later, you simply use these facts in your approach:

- *"Excuse me, Ma'am. You mentioned your daughter was going to school up north. These new jackets are the hot thing right now, and they're actually really warm and comfortable."*
- *"Sir, you said your wife likes to dress in more youthful looks. Here's a few looks from our catalog that will probably help you score some big points with her."*

These small observations are simple but powerful. Remembering one thing about your customer can help you personalize your interaction with him when you do not have time to customize it in detail. That said, don't fret if you are unable to personalize every customer encounter, even in this small way. As you've probably experienced at a theme park or a well-run movie theater, personalization is not essential to creating a great customer experience; you can provide great moments for customers without ever knowing anything about them. However, personalization *is* one of the most powerful and effective tools in the customer-facing professional's arsenal, and it's a goal that should always be in the back of your mind when interacting with a customer. In the end, it's pretty easy. All you have to do is remember one thing.

CHAPTER **37**

The Name Game
Is No Game

People love to hear their own names. It's that simple. No matter what the situation, if you are able to get a customer's name, use it. Back in 1964, Dale Carnegie wrote his personal development classic, *How to Win Friends and Influence People*. In that book, Carnegie wrote, "Remember that a person's name is to that person the sweetest and most important sound in any language."[1]

Names can be used in many ways. They can be used to pleasantly surprise the customer, like when a regular customer calls you and you spot him on caller ID. *"Thank you for calling Acme Motors. This is Stacy, and how are you today Jim?"* Names can be used to show the customer she is special and remembered. *"Welcome back, Cheryl! How are you today? Coming to check out the fall specials?"* And most important, names can be used as markers in conversations to show respect and attention. *"I understand what you're saying, Jill, and I want to assure you that I will have a solution for you by the end of the day."* By using the customer's name, you are subtly signaling that you're focused on her and her needs; you're sending a signal that you're not just reading from an invisible customer service playbook.

"But what if they don't give me a name?" I've been asked. "I feel pushy asking for it." Even on the retail floor, where many customers are strangers, names are easier to come by than you think. One trick I've developed is called the Name Delay. Here's how it works.

When you first approach the customer, you withhold your name in the initial introduction:

"Welcome to Acme. How are you today?"

"I'm fine. And you?"

"I'm spectacular! How can I assist you today?"

"I'm just looking for some jeans for my son."

"Your timing is great. We just got the new fall jeans in last week. Let me show them to you. By the way, I'm Adam."

"Oh. I'm Celia. Nice to meet you."

If you drop your name when you first approach—*"Welcome to Acme. I'm Adam. How are you today?"*—the customer will usually take that as a service rep giving his name as part of his job. But if you wait until later in the conversation and drop your name in with something like, *"By the way, I'm Adam. And you are . . . ?"* the customer views that differently. Done this way, the introduction is more conversational, more personal, and more likely to prompt the customer to give you her name in return.

Once you have a name, it's important to remember it and use it. You can easily find tricks online for remembering names. Once you master the memory part, your next goal is to use the name naturally. Some people severely overdo the name thing. I've met salespeople who've used my name in almost every sentence. *"Adam, this tire has the best mileage rating in this price range. Are you concerned with value, Adam? Let me tell you Adam, you should be."* All I can think when this is happening is, "Dude, you've been to one too many sales seminars."

Using a customer's name is a great way to personalize the customer experience and to establish rapport that can lead to easier customer interactions and more positive feelings for you and your company. Use whatever resources you have available to discover the customer's name before an interaction, and when you can't learn the name in advance, do your best to learn it during the course of the conversation. Because to a customer, his or her name truly is "the sweetest and most important sound in any language."

Notes

1. Dale Carnegie, *How to Win Friends and Influence People* (New York: Gallery, 1964), 79.

CHAPTER 38

Judge Not, Lest Ye Miss an Opportunity

A former boss of mine once told me a story. I have no idea if it's true, but it makes my point, so I'm going to use it. Let's just call it a parable. As the story goes, a family of farmers owned a large amount of acreage in the southeastern United States. Over many decades, the land increased significantly in value as one of the major cities in the South expanded and began to surround the family's property with suburbs. Eventually, part of the family's land was sold for a hefty sum to a developer who placed a large shopping mall on the property. The farmers became extremely rich.

The head of the family was an old farmer who, despite his new-found wealth, never stopped being a farmer, or looking like one. One day he went into his bank wearing overalls and dirty from his labors, and because of his appearance, the bank associates treated him poorly. At first they ignored him while they paid attention to more important-looking customers. Then they treated him in a con-descending manner when he asked to sign up for a credit card. "*You can't get a credit card without good credit. I doubt you could get approved.*"—that kind of thing. Eventually, the old farmer looked at the teller and said, "You know miss, I believe I have a bit of money in this bank. I don't appreciate the way you're talking to me, and I'd like to take my money out."

Of course, once the teller went into the farmer's account, she immediately discovered who he was and ran to get her manager. But it was too late; the damage had been done. The farmer suppos-edly pulled tens of millions of dollars in deposits from that bank, and this was back at a time when banks were not nearly as large as they are now. It was a huge loss, simply because a customer was judged by his appearance.

In Chapter 32, we examined how quickly we form impressions of others. Even the most open-minded among us form snap judgments of people subconsciously—it's how our brains are wired. However, you want to take care not to buy into judgments that might not be fair, or accurate. You want to evaluate people's potential as customers based on the information they provide that is relevant to the product or service you are offering.

Now, I'm not saying you should never make *any* judgments about anyone based on superficial or surface information. For instance, you might have to make a snap judgment for safety, like when someone walks into your bank wearing a ski mask. Also, prejudging should not be confused with prequalifying. If you work in a business where someone has to meet certain criteria to be a legitimate potential customer, then you'll likely have to prequalify prospective customers. But prequalifying is different from prejudging because it's based on information that is specifically relevant.

I've experienced this myself. I've been responsible for selling a couple of franchise opportunities in my career. The franchises required a great deal of capital to invest in, hundreds of thousands of dollars, and part of the sales process was prequalifying potential buyers. Franchising is an investment-based model, so if someone wasn't qualified or couldn't partner with someone who was, I would generally not invest much time discussing the opportunity with her. It would have been a waste of my time and the prospective franchisee's.

Prequalifying can be based on a number of criteria besides financial wherewithal. Your Olympic coaching service would not take on someone who did not have a reasonable shot at going to the Olympics. Your dog-training business might not take on a client who did not buy in to its nondominance training philosophy. My agent and publisher would not have taken me on as an author if I had not built a platform online already. In many businesses, there will be tangible reasons for prescreening or prequalifying a prospective customer based on his fit for the particular product or service. But this is not the same as prejudging based on superficial characteristics that may or may not be indicative of a customer's intent.

Most people are familiar with the famous scene in the movie *Pretty Woman* where Julia Roberts's character is dismissed by a snobbish Beverly Hills salesperson because of her appearance and then ends up spending a large amount of money at the competition. One of the reasons this chapter is important is because the *Pretty Woman* scenario is actually pretty uncommon. It's rare that a service rep will be outright rude and refuse to help someone based on appearance. What's more common are the subtle, insidious ways that service reps allow prejudgments to affect their behavior and delivery of service. When reps prejudge based on superficial appearance or past experience, they simply act differently. They'll often be pleasant, but they just won't try as hard. "*Whenever the weekend bike riders come in, all they do is order water and take up all the tables. The college kids always leave crappy tips. Don't even bother talking to the ladies in the yoga pants; they're just killing time until the class next door starts, and they never buy anything.*" Certainly, you've heard comments like these before; perhaps you've even made comments like these before. Don't feel bad; it's perfectly natural.

However, if you have outlooks like these, I recommend you ask yourself this: How does prejudging customers like this really help me? Even if there's a strain of truth in some of these judgments, what do you get out of acting on it? Maybe you get to take it a little easier since you won't be trying as hard with that customer? Perhaps you think you're teaching them a lesson? From lost sales to customers unhappy with the diminished service they receive, in most cases, prejudging customers produces negative consequences. You'll go a lot farther if you approach each new customer with a fresh outlook and an open mind.

Judge not, lest ye miss an opportunity.

CHAPTER 39

Become the Customer's Personal Detective

Your customer often needs things you do not have, and how you handle these situations can be the difference between average service and Hero-Class service. When a customer needs an item or an answer that a rep does not have, the typical response is to do a cursory check and then return with the answer. Let's say a customer has decided on a shirt she likes, but you do not have her size on the rack. The typical rep will tell the customer that all inventory is on the floor (which may or may not be true) or will go check the stockroom to see if the store has the item. Often, the process ends there. A Hero-Class rep takes it a step further; she enlists herself as the customer's own private detective.

Your goal is to come back with a solution, or at least something you can offer. If the stockroom is empty, check the online store. Check neighboring locations to see if they have it. Whatever you do, you should never come back with, *"I'm sorry, we don't have it in the back. Maybe you can find it online."* Instead, come back with, *"I apologize. We do not have your size in the store. However, I have a few options for you. How quickly do you need the piece?"*

Your goal is to have potential options ready for the customer when you return. Be creative. The options available to you might not always be giving the customer exactly what she wants but could be finding a different way to satisfy the customer's underlying need. Can you offer another model or color of the same product? Can you offer a competitive product that would actually be a better solution? Can you offer a different approach, like recommending glue instead of duct tape for a repair? Try to bear in mind that the customer is often looking for a solution to a problem. She might be willing to accept a slightly different solution than the one she had originally intended. Even if she's unwilling, you'll score major customer experience points by taking the time to offer alternatives. We'll discuss the idea of focusing on what you can do for a customer in more detail in Chapter 59.

Let's go back to our shirt example and look at how you might handle this in an actual conversation. You had asked the customer how quickly she needed the piece; you would continue by laying out the alternatives for her:

"If you need the shirt today, the fastest way would be for you to go to our Woodbridge location. If you would like, I can call over there for you to confirm that the store has the shirt, and then I can have it put aside for you. If time is not critical, I can have the shirt transferred from another location. I should have it within three days, and I can give you a call once it is in."

"I actually live pretty far from here," the customer replies, "and Woodbridge is even farther. I don't need the shirt today, but I do need it for a dinner party next Tuesday."

"I checked our online store," you respond, *"and we have the red color there. We also offer two-day shipping at no additional charge."*

"That's perfect. Thank you so much."

"Excellent! I'm glad we could find a solution for you. Let me give you the model number of the shirt because a lot of these shirts can look pretty similar online. Also, since you're already here, would you like to try on the green one to make sure you like the fit?"

As you can see from this dialogue, you can often find options to fulfill a customer's specific request. But what happens when real life is not so agreeable? What if the shirt had been discontinued and you had nothing in her size left anywhere in the company? In that situation, you would offer alternatives to the product, not alternatives on how to get the product. *"I've been recommending this Ralph Lauren piece as a great replacement for that shirt. I actually like the cuffs better on this one."*

Now, what if you have no options that directly solve the customer's issue? An example of this situation might be a specific replacement part needed to repair an old model. In this case, becoming the customer's personal detective can still pay dividends because reporting back the results of your investigation can help soften the blow when you're unable to offer any good alternatives. *"Hi, Cyndi. I apologize, but I've checked our entire system, and we don't have that part anywhere. They stopped supporting that model a few years ago. I looked everywhere I could think of. I checked our warehouse, our online store, and even called the manufacturer to see if it might have some old parts lying around. It didn't. I know you said you weren't ready to invest in a new model, but I think for the price it really might be worth it for you. However, if you have your heart set on repairing it, the best I can recommend is looking for someone selling used parts online."*

Whether you come back with a list of solid options or come back with a big fat goose egg, there will always be some customers who will not be satisfied unless they get *exactly* what they want. Don't let this tiny fraction of challenging customers prevent you from making a strong effort to become the customer's personal detective. Of course, you'll not always have time for an exhaustive search, but you should do as much as you can. You will create many more successful customer experiences and prevent a large number of service issues by pursuing every reasonable alternative to satisfy the customer. Remember, a Hero-Class rep never comes back empty-handed, even if the only thing she brings back to the customer is an explanation of how hard she tried.

CHAPTER 40

Never Talk Badly About Customers with Customers

Gossip. Bad mouthing. Trash talking. No matter what you call it, it's unprofessional and unpleasant. In Chapter 27, we discussed professionalism and touched on the negative aspects of workplace and break-room gossip. Speaking about customers negatively with coworkers is bad enough, but let's be honest, it's going to happen on occasion. Some customer situations are so crazy that you'd have to be a robot not to talk about them. However, if you feel the need to talk about a challenging customer situation with someone, there's one line you should never, ever cross: talking badly about one customer with another customer.

Speaking ill of a customer with another customer is one of the most unprofessional things you can do, and that's how your customers will view it. Even when you have a good relationship with the customer or are able to use interpersonal connection to establish rapport, this is still one boundary you should not cross. This type of situation puts the receiving customer in an uncomfortable position. What should the customer say back? How should the customer respond? When we talk about creating great customer experiences for our customers, I think we can all agree that making them uncomfortable is not what we are striving for.

This reminds me of an experience my wife and I had in the drive-through of a large coffee chain. The line was taking forever, and once we got down to the final car in front of us, the line ground to a halt. We sat there for probably five minutes watching numerous drinks go back and forth between the window and the car in front of us. When we were finally able to pull up to the window, the barista said, "That will be $9.43." Then, as he was taking the money, he seemingly changed his mind. "There's no way I'm charging you that, since you had to sit in line behind *IDIOTS!*" My wife and I burst out laughing; as unprofessional as it was, it *was* funny. Then the barista continued, "How many times can someone change their order? I confirmed it twice over the speaker, and then she changed it again at the window. What an *IDIOT!*"

The barista was as good as his word. He charged us for only one drink and left us both laughing—and horrified. In this case, the employee was more funny than angry, so that took some of the sting out of it, but in the end, the lack of professionalism stuck with us both. He was trying to do the right thing for us as customers—comping us for waiting so long—but he did it at the expense of professionalism.

You see, perhaps the most damaging part of talking badly about one customer with another customer is that the second customer naturally assumes you're talking about *him* when he's not there. Haven't we all had at least one friend in our life who talked about everyone behind their backs? After a while, didn't you just assume she was also talking trash about you when you weren't around? Of course you did, and the customer will come to a similar conclusion.

Your goal is to avoid speaking of customers in a negative way whenever possible, including with colleagues and supervisors. And no matter how intense or absurd the situation, you should never, ever speak badly about a customer with another customer. You'll find a lot of gray areas in this book and in customer service in general. Not here. This concept is black and white.

CHAPTER 41

WOW Customers in the Blink of an Eye

We've spent a lot of time so far looking at the basics of customer service, but what about service that goes above and beyond the customer's expectations? What about delivering WOW moments? While pursuing a strategy to deliver WOW customer experiences consistently (which we'll discuss further in Chapter 80) is a decision usually made by management, I think we can all agree that WOW-ing customers is generally a good thing and that you should make use of any easy opportunities you have to create above-and-beyond customer experiences.

The great news for frontline reps is that you have opportunities all around you to WOW customers with simple gestures that cost little in the way of time or money. On the Customers That Stick blog and in the CTS Service Solutions newsletter, we refer to these moments as "5-Second WOWs." Of course, these actions do not always literally take five seconds, but the name serves as a reminder that they are quick, low-effort ways to put a smile on the face of your customers and help make their experiences memorable.

Here are a few examples of 5-Second WOWs that will demonstrate how easy it is to create memorable customer experiences with only a little extra effort:

- In one of my retail service businesses, a spa, I had a regular customer who brought a Diet Coke with her every time she came in for an appointment. Each time, her service provider took the Diet Coke to the break-room refrigerator and then brought it out to the client at the end of the service.

- In 2009, my colleague Stan Phelps of 9 Inch Marketing began a project of collecting stories of customer service extras for his book *What's Your Purple Goldfish? How to Win Customers and Influence Word of Mouth,* as well as for his website of the same name. One story Stan collected was from a Realtor, who was returning a loaner car to BMW of Darien, Connecticut. When the service agent saw the Realtor pull up with his children, the agent told him to hold tight and went and got his car. Then multiple service agents helped him switch the two car seats out of the loaner. The Realtor was handed his paperwork right there at the car and told to have a nice day.[1]

- A team member of mine went to Office Depot looking for some specific clipboards she was having trouble finding. She had gone to a competitor first and received terrible service. The rep at Office Depot was attentive and personally assisted her until she was able to find what she needed. My team member told the rep how much she enjoyed going to that location and how much nicer the people there were than at the competition. The store rep asked her if she would share her comment with the rest of the Office Depot team. The store rep handed a headset to my team member, who repeated what she had just said to the entire store over the public address system. The store employees burst out in applause, and my team member felt incredibly special![2]

So what do these 5-Second WOWs really mean? What do they accomplish? Did the cold Diet Coke improve the quality of the customer's treatment? Did the assistance with the car seats make the car's engine run better? Did the announcement over the loudspeaker make the clipboards last longer? Of course not. Little WOW moments like these do not fundamentally alter the product or service you provide and, quite frankly, will not make up for a service or product that does not meet customer expectations. What these 5-Second WOWs do is create moments of connection and caring that enhance the customer's experience. These moments make the customer feel special, and they help your company stand out above the norm. When added to a consistent and well-delivered customer experience, these moments can help turn a good customer experience into a great one. Never forget that there are 5-Second WOWs all around you if you only take the time to look for them.

Notes

1. Stan Phelps, *What's Your Purple Goldfish?: How to Win Customers and Influence Word of Mouth* (9 INCH Marketing, 2012), Kindle edition, 67.

2. Donna Gurnic, "Office Depot Customer Service: Competition Is Right Next Door," Customers That Stick, November 26, 2012, http://customersthatstick.com/blog/customer-service-stories/office-depot-customer-service-competition-is-right-next-door/. Accessed August 24, 2014.

CHAPTER **42**

Customer Service Lessons Grandma Taught You

If you want to learn the most basic principles of customer service, you need ask only one person: grandma. Customer service begins and ends with the common courtesies that grandmothers have been espousing for years. While courtesy can be extended in many ways, the most obvious courtesies are communication based. They are centered on how you address another human being when you communicate with her. Do you say "Please" when you ask for her credit card? Do you say "Thank you" when she hands it to you? Do you refer to her as "Ma'am" when you address her? "Please," "Thank you," "Sir," "Ma'am," as well as similar words and phrases, are the basic building blocks of respectful communication and are the baseline for creating Hero-Class customer experiences.

Of course, this advice is incredibly obvious, and as I was writing this book, I considered whether this chapter was even necessary. However, as I continued to engage with businesses as a customer, I saw how often these simple courtesies were left out—even by reps delivering otherwise attentive and helpful service. It seems courtesy is not a universal habit, and it can be easily left out by reps who are rushed or stressed. But a lack of courtesy is never okay in customer service, and that's why it's too important a topic to be passed over.

Bear in mind also that courtesy extends beyond verbal communication to include actions as well. Greeting customers immediately or shortly after they walk through the door, holding the door for a customer, and pausing to let a customer pass are all forms of courtesy and, in my book, respect.

The keys to being consistently courteous on the service floor are awareness and habit. It's easy to get distracted, to get lost in your own world when you are busy. While you might be rushing to do something, the customer you just blew past won't always know that and may not understand why you didn't take a moment to acknowledge his presence. Courtesy is not difficult, but the Hero-Class rep makes the extra effort to pay attention to what's going on around him and takes the few additional moments necessary to be courteous to customers and colleagues alike. If you focus on making courtesy a habit, you'll find that it will quickly change from something you need to concentrate on to something you do automatically.

CHAPTER **43**

Give Your Customers Your Undivided Attention

One aspect of courtesy that seems to be getting lost in today's world is giving others our undivided attention when communicating with them. People these days are distracted by a seemingly endless assault of rings, chimes, and beeps. Mobile phones, tablets, and the Internet are all combining to rewire our brains and to change how we interact with each other. One study of college students found a direct correlation between how much they used their mobile devices and how anxious they felt.[1] Another study discovered that our attention span has been shortened so much by digital devices that the average person switches between devices 21 times an hour![2] As a result of these changes, giving customers our undivided attention and having meaningful conversations is becoming more difficult than ever.

To deliver Hero-Class customer service, you need to make sure your focus is directed at your customer. In most frontline environments, distractions abound. Intercom announcements, door chimes, and other customers, to name a few, all vie for your attention, making it easy for you to lose your focus. This doesn't mean you should become so focused on the customer that you're no longer aware of your environment. Things can happen while you're working with customers that take precedence—a small child wandering around unaccompanied, for example. However, insignificant diversions can also occur, and you shouldn't allow minor distractions to take your focus away from your mission of the moment: giving the customer your undivided attention.

Of course, it's important not only to give your customer your undivided attention but also to make sure she knows she has it.

Fortunately, a few basic techniques can help you accomplish this task easily:

- **Listen actively.** Active listening means acknowledging the customer's points by using either verbal or nonverbal cues. For instance, you can nod your head in agreement or say things like, "*I understand*," or, "*That makes sense.*"
- **Maintain eye contact.** Look the customer in the eyes while she is talking to you and show her she has your attention. Just remember to let your eyes break away on occasion, though; you don't want to creep the customer out.
- **Listen, actually.** Truly listen to what the customer is saying. This means paying attention to the point the customer is trying to get across, not just waiting for her to finish so you can speak. People can usually sense when someone is not paying attention to them, and the customer will know if you haven't done so if your responses are not on point.

In addition to the above list, the proper use of body language, which we'll discuss in the next chapter, can send an important message to the customer that you are fully engaged. If you can maintain your focus and give the customer your undivided attention, you'll find that he becomes much more agreeable and easier to work with. You'll also find that he feels respected, and that, as a result, you are in a much better position to resolve his issues, both because you formed a connection with him and because you've listened to what he has to say.

I've got to warn you, though, that giving customers your undivided attention can be frustrating at times. You should understand going into any conversation that the customer may not extend to you the same consideration or attentiveness you are giving her. The customer is having her brain rewired and attention span shortened by modern life just like you are. She might check her phone, abruptly turn her back on you to deal with her child, or simply not listen to you at all. As we have discussed previously, customer service is not a two-way street. Your job is to do your best to gain the customer's attention back and to not take her lack of attention personally.

Just remember that the customer deserves your undivided attention—even if you don't have hers.

Notes

1. Alexandra Sifferlin, "Do You Use Your Cell Phone a Lot? It Might Be Making You More Anxious," *Time,* December 6, 2013, http://healthland.time.com/2013/12/06/do-you-use-your-cell-phone-a-lot-it-might-be-making-you-more-anxious/. Accessed September 23, 2014.

2. Jennifer Smith, "Proof of Our Shrinking Attention Span: Average Person Switches Between Devices 21 Times an HOUR," Mail Online, January 5, 2014, http://www.dailymail.co.uk/news/article-2534163/Proof-shrinking-attention-span-Average-person-switches-devices-21-times-HOUR.html. Accessed September 23, 2014.

CHAPTER 44

Is Your Body Language Saying the Right Things?

Nonverbal communication is one of the most powerful forms of communication, and yet it's often overlooked by frontline reps. I've heard a frontline rep accused of providing bad service say something like, "*I told him to have a nice day*," as if the words alone were enough. Sure, he may have told the customer to have a nice day, but he did so while slouching in his chair as if it were his personal sofa and not even bothering to look up from his computer screen. Perhaps the customer didn't feel the rep's words were sincere because of the terrible nonverbal communication that accompanied them.

When I train frontline reps, I often do an experiment. I'll use a basic customer service greeting like "*Welcome to Acme Waffles. How are you today?*" On the first pass, I'll say it in a positive, energetic tone, while standing up straight. On the next pass, I'll say it sarcastically, and not even look at the rep. On the third pass, I'll say it in a low, almost depressing tone and slouch in my chair. The point of the exercise is to illustrate that the words by themselves are not enough, that other means of communication, such as tone and body language, also have a tremendous impact on how our words are delivered and received.

Multiple studies have shown that body language is a meaningful and important aspect of interpersonal communication. Albert Mehrabian, an early researcher of body language, found that the impact of a message breaks down as follows:

- 7 percent is verbal, meaning the actual words used.
- 38 percent is vocal, representing tonality and inflection of voice.
- 55 percent is nonverbal.[1]

Now, Mehrabian's research has been misinterpreted over the years. Those numbers represent the *emotional* impact of the message.[2] What you actually say matters a lot more than 7 percent in conveying your meaning, and the combination of context and the words themselves will determine how much impact your body language will have. In the training example I gave above, I was saying something essentially nice: "*Welcome to Acme Waffles. How are you today?*" And yet I was able to make it seem forced or ingenuous by changing my tone of voice and body language. However, if you were to tell a customer to "get out of my face," doing so with a happy tone of voice and a big smile probably won't make the message any less insulting. Actually, it would probably make it worse.

Research aside, there's no doubt that body language still has a huge impact on communication. How you stand, how you sit, how you gesture—all these actions send messages to the people you are communicating with. Body language is a complex topic, and I encourage you to study it in more depth, because it can only help you become a better customer service and business professional. For now, I'd like to make you aware of a few key aspects of body language that are important for frontline reps to either avoid or master:

- **Smiling.** We'll discuss smiling on the phone in Chapter 45, but it should be obvious that in face-to-face situations, smiling is an integral part of providing a welcoming experience. Just bear in mind that smiling should be used only in the proper context. If a customer is screaming at you about how bad your company screwed up, having a smile on your face while you're listening would not be appropriate.

- **Open Stance.** If we're talking to each other, my stance can tell you a lot about my interest in the conversation. If my stance is open to you, meaning that I'm primarily facing you, then I'm most likely engaged in the conversation. If my stance is closed, sort of pulling away and facing away from you, I really want to be somewhere else. Be aware of your stance when talking to customers.

- **Folded Arms.** Folding arms is typically a defensive posture (but not always). It can signal stubbornness and defensiveness, and it's generally best to avoid doing it when talking with customers. You may have noticed that many reps tend to fold their arms when listening to an upset customer; you should avoid making the same mistake. Try to keep your arms in a neutral position at your sides, except when using positive gestures while speaking.
- **Finger Pointing.** Speaking of gestures, finger pointing is aggressive and rude. You should never point at a customer. If you aren't able to control this response, I recommend getting out of frontline service as quickly as possible and finding a job where you don't have to deal with people much.
- **Good Posture.** Posture indicates many things, including confidence. You want to stand up straight when speaking with customers. If you happen to be seated, posture is even more important. You don't want to be slouched in your chair like you're watching television or hanging out with your buddies.

When thinking about the impact body language has on communication, I find it helpful to imagine being on the receiving end. Imagine you're in a conversation and the person you're speaking with is looking down at his feet or at his phone. How important would you feel? How respected? What if the person had his arms folded and was facing away from you? How engaged in what you were saying would you think he was? The answers, I should think, are similar for everyone.

When interacting with customers face-to-face, try to be aware of your body language and the signals it might be sending to your customer. Whether you take control of it or not, your body language is sending a message. The goal is to make sure it's a positive one.

Notes

1. Allan and Barbara Pease, *The Definitive Book of Body Language* (New York, Bantam, 2006), chapter excerpt in *New York Times*, Septem-

ber 24, 2006, http://www.nytimes.com/2006/09/24/books/chapters
/0924-1st-peas.html?pagewanted=all. Accessed September 23, 2014.

2. Carol Kinsey Goman, "Busting 5 Body Language Myths." *Forbes,* July
24, 2012, http://www.forbes.com/sites/carolkinseygoman/2012/07/24
/busting-5-body-language-myths/. Accessed September 23, 2014.

CHAPTER 45

Smile When You Dial

The power of nonverbal communication can extend beyond face-to-face interactions to conversations via telephone. While many nonverbal cues are lost over the phone, one important physical cue that transmits just fine is smiling. A smile over the phone might be unseen, but it is most definitely heard.

Chances are that if you are in a frontline position, you'll have to engage with customers on the phone. It's standard advice in sales and customer service to smile while doing this. In fact, there's even a term for this when applied to outgoing calls: *smile and dial*. While this advice has been around for years, it's amazing how many people have still not been exposed to it, particularly newer entrants to the workforce. It's not exactly the kind of thing they teach in school.

Interestingly, in the many times I've advised frontline reps to smile on the phone, I've never had a single person question the advice or tell me it was stupid. No one has asked whether there was research to back up the concept or accused me of promoting some sort of New Age hokum. Why? Because people intuitively know that it makes sense. Gut feelings aside, one research study took the idea a step further and demonstrated that human beings can not only differentiate vocal intonation between a smile and a nonsmile but also among different types of smiles.[1] This means customers aren't just hearing you smile but know what kind of smile it is.

So what can you do to remind yourself to smile when you're speaking with a customer on the phone? One method is to attach simple reminders to your computer monitor or the phone itself with messages like, *"Are you smiling?"* or, *"Shoulders back. Smile!"* Be sure to change the messages and their locations once in a while; otherwise, you'll get used to seeing them and they'll lose their impact.

Another great tip is to set up a small mirror near the phone so you can see yourself as you speak. I know of one company that places branded mirrors at each phone rep's station so the reps can see if they are smiling when they are on the phone.

While these ideas might not always be possible in shared phone situations or without manager approval, they are both great ways for you to remind yourself to smile when speaking to customers on the phone.

Another technique I like to use to help convey energy and emotion over the phone is standing up. If I have an important phone call or if I just happen to feel my energy sagging, I stand up. A lot of other executives and professionals I know do so as well. You're simply more confident and more energetic when standing, and I believe that comes across over the phone. Besides, sitting too much is bad for you, so why not stand up more?[2]

Now that you know how important it is to smile (and stand) when you dial, let's look at the specific ways you can adapt your communication to the unique challenges of working with customers over the phone.

Notes

1. University of Portsmouth, "Smile—And the World Can Hear You, Even If You Hide," ScienceDaily, January 16, 2008, http://www.science daily.com/releases/2008/01/080111224745.htm. Accessed September 23, 2014.

2. Juststand.org, "The Facts: Sit-Stand Basics," http://www.juststand .org/tabid/816/default.aspx. Accessed October 25, 2014.

CHAPTER 46

The Phone Is Different, and the Same

When you remove body language and facial expressions from communication, you remove many of the signals we use to read other people. Communication over the phone leaves you and your customer with limited insight into how the person on the other end of the conversation is reacting. Is he in a defensive posture and getting more withdrawn as you talk? Is she rolling her eyes while you tell her how much you value her business? Is he reading his email instead of listening to you? The more physical cues we remove from our interactions, the easier it is to have misunderstandings. Fortunately, as we learned in Chapter 45, you can still tell a lot from tone of voice. Unfortunately, the situation gets much worse when we talk about email and social media, which we'll discuss in Part Nine.

The challenges of phone communication don't change the fact that the majority of customer service principles you use face-to-face can be used on the phone as well, sometimes with just slight modifications. For instance, you generally don't want to interrupt your customer when he's talking (except when you do; see Chapter 62 for more on that); on the phone, it's no different, except that it's more difficult to know when the person is finished speaking. You can't use eye contact and body language to help convey the message that you're paying attention, so you have to ramp up your active listening a bit to get the point across. You have to communicate through voice what you can't communicate through presence. *"Yes, Ma'am. I understand. I'm so sorry to hear that."*

The phone also magnifies pauses and absences. The customer on the other end of the phone is blind to what you're doing. In a physical environment, the customer can see you walk to the back of the store to check for an item; on the phone, all he will hear is dead air. In a physical environment, the customer can watch you actively looking for an item on your computer; on the phone, the customer doesn't know if you are working on his case or went to grab coffee. One of the fundamental concerns with telephone communication is making sure that you do not pull Service Trigger #2: Being Abandoned. As we learned when discussing that trigger in Chapter 16, overcommunication is a key technique for preempting and addressing this challenge, and it's crucial when working with customers via telephone.

On the phone, the goal is to minimize dead air, both in conversation and when the customer is on hold. To do this, you simply need to communicate at regular intervals. You shouldn't be ridiculous about it—*"I'm moving my cursor now; I'm clicking over to screen two"*—but you do want to reassure the customer that you're actively engaged in the process. *"Okay, I just sent the request. It can take up to 90 seconds for an approval."* After 45 seconds or so, you can check in again. *"I just wanted to let you know that I'm still waiting on the approval; it should be here soon."*

The same principles apply when a customer is on hold. People perceive time differently when they're actively doing something versus passively waiting. How much quicker does time pass when you're playing your favorite sport versus when you are in a doctor's office waiting room? That's the difference between how you feel while actively working on an issue and how the customer feels waiting for you to do so, and that is why it's so important to regularly check back in with a customer who is on hold.

An additional challenge that stems from the interpersonal gap created by phone communication is that it can embolden customers to act less politely than they might in person. On the phone, a customer can feel protected and a bit anonymous and will, quite frankly, be more likely to yell or say something harsh than he would face-to-face. Particularly in situations where you don't have a previous relationship with the customer, you can be viewed as just a nameless, abstract service rep and not a flesh-and-blood person. We'll work on how to handle challenging customers, wherever you might encounter them, in Part Seven. For now, just be aware that this is an additional dynamic when working with customers over the phone.

The good news is that while the differences discussed in this chapter are important to note and to work around, customer service on the phone is not tremendously different from what it is face-to-face. Many of the techniques and concepts you have learned and will learn in this book apply in both situations. As long as you're aware of the differences noted here, you should have the tools you need to handle most situations with ease.

CHAPTER 47

Use BRWY Communication

In Chapter 17, we looked briefly at Be Right With You (BRWY) communication, the act of telling customers things like, *"I'll be right with you,"* or, *"I'll be with you in a moment,"* when you're unable to engage with them immediately. This technique is a potent antidote to customers feeling ignored by service reps who are tied up with other customers or activities.

Most customers are understanding if you're speaking with another customer or are tied up on the phone, and they usually don't expect you to immediately break away and help them. Mostly, they just want to be acknowledged; they want to know they're not being ignored and that you know they're there. We've already discussed what a powerful trigger being ignored is, and it's important to recognize that the fear of being unnoticed can be just as potent. When a customer wonders if you're aware of her presence, what she's really wondering is if you're going to waste her time. Are you going to take an extra-long time with the current customer because you don't know she is waiting? Are you going to walk off after your phone conversation because you didn't see her? When you take a moment to acknowledge a customer, you help eliminate this stress and fear, create a more relaxed customer, and set the stage for a more pleasant and positive interaction.

BRWY communication can take many forms and be used effectively in a variety of situations. When you're behind the cash wrap and on the phone, you can subtly cover the mouthpiece and say, *"I'll be with you in just a moment."* When you're speaking with another customer face-to-face, you can simply wait for a natural pause in the conversation, say, *"Excuse me,"* to the customer you're speaking with, and tell the waiting customer, *"We should just be a couple of more minutes."*

Of course, you have to use your judgment. Breaking your attention from a current customer, even if just for a flash, is not always advisable. If the conversation you're having is with an irate customer, you should probably not pause to acknowledge the customer who's waiting. Don't worry; if the waiting customer can hear the exchange, he's likely to be more than understanding. If the situation is not good for BRWY language, that's okay. Sometimes all you need is a quick nod of the head, eye contact, and a smile to let a customer know you've seen him.

As we discussed in Chapter 46, when a customer is on hold, it's important to check back in and let him know you're not ignoring him or have not forgotten about him. This is where BRWY communication can be very effective. *"Hi, I just wanted to check back in with you to let you know that I'm still tied up on the previous call. I should only be a few more minutes. Would you like to hold or can I take your name and number and give you a call back?"* Again, the same caveats apply to using BRWY communication on the phone. You might not be able to break away from your current interaction to do so, but when you're able to, you should.

It is important to note that BRWY communication is only effective when you're doing something the customer believes to be a legitimate priority—for example, helping a customer who was there first or putting down a caution sign for a water spill. The technique is meaningless if the customer can see you participating in an activity she does not believe takes precedence over her needs—for example, talking to a coworker or checking your mobile phone. Even if both actions are legitimately work related, they may not seem that way. Always remember that the customer's perception is what dictates the customer's experience.

Customer perception is one of the reasons BRWY communication is so powerful. Acknowledging a customer who's waiting might not mean that you're going to move any faster with your current customer, but the customer will likely perceive that you are. By acknowledging the customer's presence, you send her a signal that you're working to get to her, that you know she is waiting, and that you will not take more time than necessary completing what you are currently engaged with.

BRWY communication is one of the easiest and strongest proactive service techniques in the customer-facing professional's arsenal. It helps start a customer's experience off on the right note, replacing uncertainty with assurance and giving the customer a feeling of value and recognition.

CHAPTER 48

Want to Help Your Customers? Shut Up

There are two words of advice that all good customer service reps and salespeople know: shut up. Learning to be quiet when a customer is talking is one of the many areas where customer service and sales are remarkably similar. When confronted with a prospect or a customer who has an issue, the initial reaction of most service reps is to start talking, offering assistance, and attempting to avoid the discomfort of silence. Salespeople do it too, throwing out everything they know about a product and hoping a shotgun approach will work. Both the customer service rep and the salesperson innately feel that if they're talking, then they must be helping the customer. More often than not, they're making it worse.

Let's take an example from the sales world and then look at how the principle applies to customer service. One of my favorite television shows is *Shark Tank*, where small-business owners pitch a group of wealthy investors for business funding. The ideas are for real businesses, and the investors invest their own funds if they like a concept. I watched an episode a few years ago in which a very confident gentleman was attempting to secure an investment in his corporate sales training program. In his pitch, he described himself as an "expert sales professional" and claimed he could "sell anything to anyone"—a pretty gutsy claim to make in a roomful of high-powered investors.[1]

The funny part was that after a pitch filled with aggressive performance claims, one of the "sharks," Daymond John, handed the gentleman a pen and gave him an age-old interview-role-playing scenario: sell me this pen. Now, in one of my retail businesses, we've used a version of this forever, so I have a very good idea of the type of response to look for. What I look for is questions. On the front end, questions should be used to identify what the prospect needs: *"Before I tell you about my line of pens, Daymond, let me ask you, what qualities are you looking for in a pen?"* But what do most people do? They immediately start rambling about features. *"What you'll like about our pen is that it is stainless steel. . . ."* If they are lucky, they might stumble onto a benefit: *"This means your pen won't corrode. I know you live in a humid climate . . ."* The people who knock the pen challenge out of the park ask questions first, then shut up and listen.

What did the "expert sales professional" do? He hardly asked Daymond a single question, and in fact, another "shark," Mark Cuban, had to chime in to push the salesperson to try to close the sale. Instead of using careful questioning and active listening to elicit what his prospect wanted (at least as the show's editors portrayed it), the gentleman kept talking in the hopes that something he said would eventually address the prospect's need. This rarely works, in sales or in customer service.

There's an old expression in sales: telling is not selling. Well, in customer service, talking is not solving. When a customer shares an issue with you, you have two choices: Act on the information or probe for clarification. Sometimes the problem is simple enough that further clarification isn't needed, but for most situations, asking questions is the best way to start. It's the difference between these two approaches: *"I'm so sorry that you feel the cashier was rude to you. That cashier is one of our best blah, blah, blah,"* or, *"I'm so sorry that you feel the cashier was rude to you. Can you tell me a little bit about what happened so I can assist you with this?"*

In the first scenario, we've begun providing every reason we can think of and hoping one of them sticks, instead of clarifying what it is the client feels or wants. Sure, we know the customer was aggrieved in some way by the cashier, but we have not delved into what that really means to her. In the second scenario, we've given her a chance to be heard. We've shown that we care about what she feels—half the battle—and we're gaining valuable information on how to really address her needs in the process.

We'll delve into the importance of asking questions in Chapter 49, but for now, please bear in mind that one of the most important lessons you can learn in customer service is to shut up. If you let the customer do most of the talking and you actually listen to what she is saying, the few words you do use will be more effective and will resonate with the customer far more.

Notes

1. ABC, *Shark Tank*, season 3, episode 2.

Ask Questions, Lots of Questions

Questions are at the core of Hero-Class customer service. Without questions, everything in customer service is harder. It's more difficult to find out what's really bothering the customer or what the customer expects from his experience. It's more challenging to show interest in the customer or to indicate that we care. Yet for far too many frontline reps, answers are the first reaction to any customer service interaction. As we learned in Chapter 48, talking is not solving, and unless what the customer wants is cut and dried, using questions professionally and effectively is almost always the best way to work through a customer interaction.

While it's impossible to cover all the ways you can use questions in customer service, here are a few ideas to help you get into an inquisitive mindset when interacting with customers. The list will serve as a good reference source as you focus on using questions more actively in your frontline interactions. Depending on the situation, discovering many of the following things about your customers can be useful:

- What the customer likes
- What the customer needs
- Whom at your company the customer has worked with before
- What the customer's experience has been with your company
- What the customer's experience has been with your product or service
- What the customer's experience has been with the competition
- What the customer's experience has been with similar products

- How the customer feels about your company or product
- What the customer intends to use the product for
- What the customer's expectations are
- How the company did not meet the customer's expectations
- What it will take to resolve the customer's issue
- What it will take to regain the customer's business

As the list above demonstrates, there's likely a lot you do not know about the customer standing in front of you. Information is powerful, and the more you can learn that's relevant to satisfying and even delighting the customer, the better positioned you'll be to create Hero-Class customer experiences.

A word of caution. Like almost every concept we discuss in this book, questions can be ineffective when poorly asked or taken to extremes. Do not become so question focused that you make the customer feel like she is being interrogated. Good conversation travels in both directions, and the customer is looking for information from you as well. She wants to know what happened, why it happened, and what you're going to do about it. She does not want to be cross-examined; she wants to be understood and to have her needs met or issues resolved. Questions are simply the best way to accomplish those things for her.

The topic of questions is very broad, and we are only able to touch on some basic concepts in a single chapter. The idea I urge you to take away from this discussion is just how important questions are. As you read through dialogue examples in the remainder of the book, you'll notice how often questions are used in interacting with customers and particularly in working with difficult situations. You'll be able to use these questions in your own service interactions and customize them for your own job.

CHAPTER 50

Jargon Is a Wall Between You and the Customer

When you use jargon that a customer is unfamiliar with, you create a wall between you and your customer. What is jargon? It's the inside language of your industry or your company. It's the language you use every day that most of your customers are probably not familiar with.

Jargon can come in a variety of forms. Acronyms are notorious sources of jargon. While your customer surely knows what the acronyms IRS or FBI stand for, she probably doesn't know that your computer system is called a CID system or that your purchasing software is called your DLS system. Nonobvious titles or departments are also big sources of jargon. When you refer to your manager or your accounting department, most customers can relate to these terms, but when you refer to your cross-functional expediter or your digital procurement department, you're going to see your customer's eyes glaze over.

The use of jargon has to be proactively guarded against because it's habitual. It's a form of tribal communication that you and your teammates use to communicate as effectively and efficiently as possible. But for customers, the language is neither effective nor efficient. In the best case, the customer will simply not understand what you are talking about; in the worst case, the customer will feel you are talking down to him.

Let's look at two examples of communicating with a customer; the first uses jargon, and the second says the same thing using everyday language:

- *"I apologize, Ma'am. Our DLS system is experiencing a buffering issue. Our IT department is going to send out a CRT team in the next two hours. I should be able to synchronize your records once it's back online."*
- *"I apologize, Ma'am. Our computer system is down, and I can't access your records at this time. Our computer folks are saying it should be up within the next two hours. I should be able to get you the information as soon as they have it working again."*

Which of these forms of communication do you think the customer would be more likely to respond to positively? Which form do you think has the least possibility to make the customer feel disconnected from your company and possibly even insulted by you?

Jargon does not make the speaker seem important; it just makes him seem distant and hard to relate to. Jargon is nothing more than a wall between you and your customers. Always speak to your customers in plain language, and leave the jargon for your TPS reports.

CHAPTER 51

10 Power Words You Must Use

If there are words and acronyms like jargon that you do not want to use because the meaning will be unclear to customers, then it stands to reason there are words that have the opposite effect, that are virtually guaranteed to convey a clear and understandable message. While all words can mean different things to different people, some words are powerful not because of their specific meaning but because they have the same general impact on most people who hear them. *Love* is an example of such a word. It means different things to different people, but in the great majority of cases, telling someone you love her will elicit a strong, positive response.

On the front lines, having a store of power words that you can incorporate into your vocabulary can help you not only create richer customer experiences when all is well but can also help you more easily address challenging situations. Here are 10 power words that can be useful to any customer-facing professional:

1. "Appreciate." This word speaks for itself. Everyone likes to feel appreciated, and this word can and should be used liberally in a variety of contexts. *"I appreciate your patience." "We truly appreciate your business." "I appreciate your willingness to give us a chance to correct the issue for you."*

2. "Respect." As we discussed in Chapter 22, the concept of respect can be hard to pin down. Yet the *word* "respect" almost always creates a positive impact on the listener. *"I completely respect what you are saying." "I truly respect and appreciate the fact that you took time to bring this to our attention."*

3. "Accountability." This is a positive word that signals your willingness (and your organization's willingness) to be accountable. *"I understand, and I am accountable for that." "We absolutely are accountable for that mistake, and I am going to do everything I can to make it right for you."* Accountability can also be used in situations where you need to stand up to a customer, and it can be a nice way of letting a customer know the situation is not entirely the company's fault. *"We are willing to take accountability for the late delivery, but we confirmed the part number three times and have your signed purchase order."* (See use of "but" statements in Chapter 72.) *"We are certainly willing to be held accountable for the places we dropped the ball in this situation, and I want to make sure we can find a workable solution."*

4. "Understand." Who doesn't want to be understood? Empathy is an important part of any customer-facing role, and no word conveys empathy more universally than "understand." *"I understand why you're upset." "I understand how you feel." "I understand how the promotion could be read that way."*

5. "Committed." We'll look at the idea of assuring accountability in Chapter 52. At the heart of that technique is the idea of committing oneself to the customer—whether to facilitate his customer experience or to resolve his issue. Using the word "commitment," when you're willing and able to live up to it, can send a strong signal to a customer. *"I am committed to sticking with you until this issue is resolved." "I will commit to getting the part to you by Thursday, even if I have to hand it to our delivery driver myself."*

6. "Absolutely." Don't just say yes—say absolutely! Whenever you can do something for a customer, you lose nothing by agreeing to it with some positivity and enthusiasm. *"Can you have the alterations done by Tuesday? Absolutely!"* If you like, you can substitute "definitely" or "certainly." Simply find a word you are comfortable with and kick it up a notch from just saying yes!

7. "Suggest." "Suggest" is a soft word that has tremendous power. It helps you direct the customer while giving him a feeling of control. It's nice way of telling a customer he needs to do something. "Suggest" is not a word to use when you need to be firm with a customer but, instead, when you want to soften an unwanted message. *"I'm going to suggest that you upgrade to the latest version of our software." "Based on the level of wear, we strongly suggest you replace your front two tires."*

8. "Option." Everyone likes having options; no one likes being boxed in. The word "option" is extremely powerful when you're unable to provide exactly what the customer is looking for. *"One option would be for me to call the store over in Richland for you." "Here is an option I think you will like."*

9. "Challenge." This word is a great substitute for the word "problem." It's softer and has the connotation of something that's more easily handled than a problem. Sometimes you can use it when discussing the customer's problems; you can almost always use it when discussing yours or the company's. For instance, if a customer is upset about an ongoing service issue, you might not want to soft pedal the situation by saying something like, *"I understand your challenge."* On the other hand, you, the service rep, never have problems; you only have challenges. *"The challenge is that we don't manufacture that part ourselves, and there is a serious shortage since the typhoon in Asia last month." "The only real* *challenge I am going to have is getting the item in before Christmas."* If you used "problem" instead of "challenge" in those last two sentences, they would have sounded more negative.

10. "Solution." Everyone wants problems to be solved, challenges to be overcome, and issues to be resolved. The magic word that makes them feel all of the above has happened is "solution." *"Great news! I've found the perfect solution for the static you've been getting from that microphone." "I have a few different solutions that I would like to present for your consideration."* When you use the word "solution," you send a message that you have solved the customer's problem.

The list above is by no means all-inclusive. Many more words are useful and effective in frontline service roles. You'll see many of them scattered throughout this book in phrases and examples. However, the list represents a nice, digestible bite of universally powerful service words.

Learn to incorporate the words in this list into your service vocabulary, but beware of overuse in any individual situation that might come across as insincere. Used in a timely and authentic fashion, these power words can help you create more effective and impactful conversations with customers and colleagues.

CHAPTER 52

Assure Accountability

As we learned in Chapter 16, customers fear few things in customer service more than being abandoned by an organization. It's one of the most common and resonant of the Seven Service Triggers. Yet no matter how much you try to avoid it, you'll have to disengage from customers on occasion. You may need to pass the issue on to another department, to research the issue further, or to elevate the issue to a supervisor or manager. In the real world, it happens.

For many customers, the moment you say you're going to disengage from conversation is the moment their states change. The customer who is already upset that the issue is not being resolved at that moment now becomes concerned that he will be abandoned. He has been blown off by so many organizations before, perhaps even your own, that he immediately fears that no one, including you, is going to call him back. To allay this fear and to help the customer feel confident when disengaging, one of the best techniques I know of is assuring accountability. We touched on this idea briefly in Chapter 17, but let's take a deeper dive into how to effectively use this technique to preempt and overcome abandonment issues.

To begin, the mere act of your taking responsibility for the customer is a positive action that will go a long way toward allaying the customer's fear and distrust. Consider the difference between the following two scenarios:

- *"Sir, I have to check with my procurement department for that. They should get back to me within three business days. I can call you as soon as I hear from them."*
- *"Sir, I'm going to have to check with my procurement department to get you a firm answer, but I want you to know that*

I'm going to personally make sure you get an answer to your question. It can take them up to three business days, but I'll do my best to push it through faster. How about if I commit to getting back to you by close of business Wednesday and giving you a status update either way?"

The first response wasn't necessarily bad. It was the truth, it was professional, and it promised a follow-up. What it didn't do was give the customer confidence that this experience would be different from the 20 other experiences he's had when a service rep said he would call and never did. That's exactly what the second scenario did.

Now let's look at a few specific ways you can significantly increase the effectiveness of this technique:

- **Assure personal responsibility.** You want to use phrases and words that give the customer a sense that you are on her side, that you have taken ownership of her issue. You might not be the one to solve it, but you should be the one to make sure she is kept in the loop. Use phrases like, *"I am going to personally make sure,"* or, *"I am going to commit to you,"* to let the customer know you plan to stick with her to the end.

- **Give a firm date for your next contact.** Always commit to a specific date by when you will contact the customer. You're not committing to a resolution, particularly if the solution is not in your control, but you are committing to give her a status update. *"I'm not sure if I'll have the answer by then, but I'll make sure to check in with you Thursday either way to let you know what is happening."*

- **Get or verify contact information.** Always confirm the best contact method, even if you already have it. The mere act of confirming this information sends a signal to the customer that you're serious about what you've said. Also, sometimes you'll get a different answer than you expect, and you don't want to work hard to resolve the issue only to drop the ball because you didn't have the right contact info.

Perhaps one of the most important aspects of assuring accountability is this: Be first. If you wait until the customer has already jumped all over you with questions, half the battle is lost. *"When will someone call me back? Who will call me back? What do I do if someone doesn't call me back?"* If the customer has to pull the information from you, you've already pulled her abandonment trigger and put her on the defensive about the entire situation. You want to proactively provide the assurance and accountability the customer seeks before she can slip into abandonment and distrust. Give her the information she needs before she asks.

I know many of you reading this may not be in a position to assure accountability, specifically in some of the ways used in the examples above. One of the methods I teach, especially for dealing with really upset or distrustful customers, is to offer to send an email confirming what the rep has committed to. It works wonders, because most people are much more comfortable knowing they'll have something in writing if things go wrong down the road.

But what if you work the service floor and don't have access to email in your job? What if you don't have access to a calendar at work to remind you to follow up on Thursday? What if you're leaving for vacation on Monday for a week? No matter what your position, you'll have times when you're unable to fully assure accountability for a customer issue. In such situations, simply assume as much accountability as possible. *"Ma'am, I just want to let you know that I'll be on vacation next week; however, I'm going to personally make sure my manager sees this today. If you haven't heard from him by end of day Monday, please call. His name is Bill Smith, and he can be reached here at the store."*

One of the nice features of assuring accountability is that it can be an effective technique even when you're not fully disconnecting from the customer. Let's say you have to check the stockroom for an item. Generally, you wouldn't need to assure accountability; however, with an upset customer, such language can soothe him a bit when you have to disconnect temporarily. *"I understand, Sir; you have every reason to be upset. We absolutely should have called you about the special order. I have to go to the back to see if it came in with this morning's delivery, but let me just assure you that I'm going to get to the bottom of this for you."*

Additionally, assuring accountability can also provide an extra level of attention and rapport building, even when not disconnecting. *"The computer is showing four of those items. Let's take a walk over to that department together, and I'll stick with you until we find them."* Certainly, you don't need to assure accountability in this situation, but it still has a powerful effect psychologically on the customer. You've placed yourself on the customer's team, and she can feel good that she has an ally in her quest, no matter how inconsequential.

When done well, assuring accountability is one of the most powerful weapons in the Hero-Class service rep's arsenal. Used properly, it can give customers a sense of confidence that they have a champion on their side; it can help the customer feel that just because you're disconnecting, that doesn't mean you're disappearing.

CHAPTER 53

Always Get Buy-In for Your Response Times

As we discussed in Chapter 17, one of the most powerful techniques when disengaging from a customer is getting buy-in for your response time. This is an easy concept: You're simply asking the customer if the date or time you want to get back to her by is acceptable. The power of this process is that it gives the customer a sense of control and input. How can she get angry about you not calling her back until Thursday when she said it was okay? Once the customer agrees, even if only grudgingly, she has buy-in on the timeline. This helps take pressure off both you and her, and it's the perfect technique to combine with assuring accountability to make disengaging from customers as smooth as possible. Here's how these two techniques might work together:

> *"Mary, I just spoke with my manager, and she said she'll have to wait until accounting gets in on Monday to get the account details. I apologize that I can't solve the issue for you at the moment, but I want to make sure we're able to give you a solution that will turn this experience around for you. How about if I give you a call on Tuesday to follow up? If I get an answer sooner than that, either my manager or I will call you, but if we don't have a resolution by then, I'll personally call you on Tuesday to give you a status update. Does Tuesday work for you?"*

As you can see from this example, when you can combine taking personal accountability with getting buy-in from the customer on response time, you send a message that gives the customer confidence that she won't be abandoned or forgotten once you disengage from her.

Since this book is all about customer service in the real world, we need to discuss the fact that on occasion, the customer might not agree to your response time. What happens then? To be prepared for this possibility and to give yourself a little extra time for unforeseen circumstances, I recommend adding a little padding in your initial approach. Simply embrace the old customer service adage of under-promise, overdeliver. Make sure you leave yourself enough time so you not only have a high probability of resolving the issue for the customer, but hopefully have enough time that you can get back to her ahead of schedule. Either way, the padding can serve you well by giving you a fallback position in the initial conversation:

> *"Mary, I certainly understand, and I only recommended Tuesday because I wanted to make sure I had enough time to get a solution for you. Your issue is a priority for me, and I'm going to make sure it's on the top of my manager's to-do pile on Monday morning. How about if I give you a call toward the end of the day Monday to give you an update? I'm not sure I'll have an answer by then, but I hope to."*

When combined with assuring accountability, getting buy-in for your response time is the one-two punch in dealing with customer abandonment fears. Used separately or together, both techniques will go a long way toward making disengagement from customers much smoother.

CHAPTER 54

Don't Make Promises
You Can't Keep

Having just discussed the topics of assuring accountability and getting buy-in for response times, we should take a brief look at one of the most fundamental principles in customer service: Don't make promises you can't keep. Don't give a response time you're unlikely to meet. Don't assure accountability if you don't have the ability to follow through. Don't tell the customer you can shepherd her project through to completion if you're going on vacation for a week or your company policy won't allow you to. Make sure you can deliver.

Of course, this principle extends to everything you do in customer service, and let me be the first to admit that it's often easier said than done. Often you'll be in a situation where you really don't know what you can commit to. You don't know if the part will be in on time. You don't know if the billing department will get back to you by Tuesday. You don't know if your manager will let you waive company policy to resolve the issue. I'm sure you've been there before. You're in a bind. You want to avoid making a promise you can't keep, but you also want to give the customer something concrete that makes him feel confident about what will happen next.

The best advice I can give you for situations like these is to have an honest but carefully worded conversation with the customer. One advantage of being on the front lines is that customers usually understand that you have limited control over things outside your immediate area. While you don't want to come across as making excuses, you should be honest about when you can't commit to something. When you're in this position and you are able, the best thing to do is to assure accountability, not for the outcome, but, at the least, for communicating with the customer. No matter what, you'll always have situations where you have to find that balance between seeming slippery by not committing to anything and making promises you aren't sure you can keep.

CHAPTER **55**

The Art of the Pivot

When he was running for president in 1992, Bill Clinton had a list of three fundamental campaign messages posted on the wall of his campaign headquarters:

1. "Change versus more of the same"
2. "The economy, stupid"
3. "Don't forget health care"[1]

These three messages embodied the heart of what the Clinton campaign wished to convey to the country, which it did to the tune of a successful presidential election.

How was the Clinton campaign able to convey its message so effectively? One reason was the rhetorical skill of the candidate himself. Among President Clinton's most estimable political skills, recognized by friend and foe alike, was his ability to pivot almost any discussion to one of his key campaign themes. Ask him about military preparedness, and by the time he got to the end of the answer, he was discussing the economy. Ask him about Western water rights, and he would pivot from that to clean water and from that to health care. Pivoting is not just useful for politicians, however. It's the ability to direct a conversation to where you want it to go and, as such, it can be an incredibly powerful tool to have in your customer service tool belt.

I've found that many customer-facing professionals lack the ability to pivot well. Why? Because they respond to questions the way most conscientious people do—by trying to directly answer the question they were asked. And by continuing to answer the question they were asked. And then answering it some more. If the question is a productive one—"*What are you going to do about this?*"—then pivoting often isn't necessary. However, if the question is one that keeps the conversation in a negative place or is simply unproductive—"*Is it your whole company or just you that's incompetent?*"—then pivoting can help you shift the conversation to more productive territory.

Here's a quick example of pivoting in a typical customer service situation. Let's say the customer asks, "*Why didn't your salesperson explain to me that the sale ended yesterday when I called her this morning? Because of her, I drove 40 minutes for nothing.*"

"*I certainly understand, Ma'am. It's obvious that information would have prevented this situation and your driving all the way down here. But since you are here, let me help you make the best out of this situation now. What I can do for you is . . .*"

As you can see from that example, you aren't avoiding accountability but are shifting the conversation to more productive ground. The customer is focused on what went wrong in the past; you want her focused on how it's going to be better in the present.

Following are a few specific pivoting techniques you can begin to incorporate into your own customer communication. While they're similar in effect, each one provides a slightly different approach, which can be tailored to the individual circumstances. For brevity's sake, these examples assume you've already acknowledged the situation and have gotten to the point where you are ready to move the conversation forward:

- **Time Pivot.** Like the scenario above, you want to help move the customer from focusing on what happened in the past to what you can do for him in the present. "*Let's talk about what I can do for you today.*" "*Let me tell you a few options I have available right now.*"
- **Best-Way Pivot.** This pivot incorporates a framing technique in which you try to move the conversation to a place that's superior to where it currently stands. "*The best way for me*

to help you is . . ." "Let me tell you the best way that I can resolve this issue for you."

- **Permission Pivot.** In this situation, you signal your desire to move the conversation forward by asking permission to shift the discussion. *"Would you mind if I asked you a question?" "Do you mind if I present you with a few options?"* This pivot is less effective with a customer who is really upset, but it's a soft way to pivot customers who can't seem to get focused on a solution.

- **Social-Proof Pivot.** This pivot uses the idea of social proof to help create interest in allowing you to move the conversation forward. *"I had a situation similar to yours recently, and I was able to find a great solution for the customer." "I found a great solution to a similar situation a few weeks ago; I think you'll like it."*

- **Intention Pivot.** Here, you simply use your intention to help the customer as a pivot point in the conversation. *"My goal is to turn this situation around for you; let me tell you . . ." "I want to make this right for you; here are a few options . . ."*

When done well, pivots can be tremendously effective; however, when done poorly, pivoting can make a service rep seem cagy or dishonest. In a poorly executed pivot, it's obvious that the rep is not even attempting to answer the question he was asked or addressing what the customer is upset about. You want to avoid seeming like a slippery politician. Effective pivoting is not about avoiding questions or accountability; it's about not allowing the conversation to stay mired in the muck of problems.

Since pivoting is a skill that doesn't come naturally for most people, the best way to master it is to practice it without a customer. To start, I recommend writing down the top customer complaints your company receives and then experimenting with different types of pivots to see which ones are most effective. Focus on memorizing a handful of transitional phrases that you feel comfortable with, and get used to using those in real-world situations. By mastering three to five go-to phrases you can use in most situations, you'll find yourself much more effective in moving customer conversations to productive ground.

Notes

1. Michael Kelly, "The 1992 Campaign: The Democrats—Clinton and Bush Compete to Be Champion of Change; Democrat Fights Perceptions of Bush Gain," *New York Times,* October 31, 1992, http://www .nytimes.com/1992/10/31/us/1992-campaign-democrats-clinton-bush-compete-be-champion-change-democrat-fights.html. Accessed August 24, 2014.

PART SEVEN

MASTER DIFFICULT SITUATIONS

CHAPTER **56**

Complaints Should Come with Bows on Them

We've focused a lot on mindset so far, and as we embark upon the topic of mastering difficult situations, one of the best things you can do as a frontline professional is to begin viewing complaints positively. Let's not kid ourselves—complaints, particularly the really unpleasant ones, suck. No one likes to receive them, because implicit in most complaints is the accusation that either you or your organization have failed the customer. Who wants to hear that?

Yet there's another side to complaints that bears consideration: What happens when a customer doesn't complain? In general, the answer is: nothing good. Silent attrition—when customers leave but never say a word to the company—is a huge issue in many businesses. According to Andrea J. Ayers of Convergys, which sells customer and information management products, companies lose 12 percent of their customers, averaged across industries, to silent attrition. In the credit card industry, the number is 43 percent![1] Even worse, the customer isn't actually silent. He's telling plenty of people about the bad experience he had; he's just not telling you. And that's why complaints are important. When the customer tells you what's wrong, no matter how unpleasant, he's giving you an opportunity to bond with him, to learn what his issues are, and to hopefully resolve the issue and save the relationship. This is an opportunity that silence does not provide.

In *A Complaint Is a Gift*, authors Janelle Barlow and Claus Moller flip the traditional idea that complaints are something to be feared on its head. They contend that complaints should be welcomed and that organizations can gain from complaints in many ways, including understanding what is important to their customers and getting ideas for improving new products and services. Barlow and Moller offer this explanation:

> In simplest terms, complaints are statements about expectations that have not been met. They are also, and perhaps more importantly, opportunities for an organization to reconnect with customers by fixing a service or product breakdown. In this way, complaints are gifts customers give to businesses. Everyone will benefit from carefully opening these packages and seeing what is inside.[2]

This concept gives us an excellent way to reframe complaints; the challenge is embracing this idea on the front lines, when a customer is expounding on the many ways your organization has failed him and ruined not only his day but his entire month. We'll discuss techniques and language for handling complaints as we work through Parts Seven and Eight, but the most important place to begin is by remembering that no matter the intensity or the complexity of the complaint, it has value to you and your organization. Because in the end, how you view a complaint is a pretty good indication of how you'll handle one.

Notes

1. Andrea J. Ayers, "Executives Have No Idea What Customers Want," *Forbes,* March 10, 2009, http://www.forbes.com/2009/03/10/con sumers-executives-disconnect-leadership-managing-convergys.html. Accessed September 23, 2014.

2. Janelle Barlow and Claus Moller, *A Complaint Is a Gift* (Berrett-Koehler, 2008), digital edition, 75.

CHAPTER 57

Listening Is a Start, Understanding Is the Goal

In Chapter 48, we discussed the importance of shutting up and listening to customers when they speak. Listening, however, is only half the battle; understanding is the real goal, and this is never more important than when working with an unsatisfied or upset customer. Listening is not always the same as understanding, because a customer won't always tell you what she means, what's really bothering her, or what you need to know to address her issue. Imagine that a customer says to you, *"I've had it up to here with this stuff. Every time I come in here, you people screw things up."* What do you really understand about the customer's issue? You know the customer believes the company has screwed up repeatedly. But screwed up what or how? What expectation has not been met? You simply don't have enough information.

Or let's say a customer is angry because her lunch order is taking too long. She says she's in a rush, but after speaking with her, you realize she only ordered three minutes ago, which is not long at all in your restaurant. You can understand why she might be a bit agitated, but she's off the charts, boiling mad. She says she's mad about the time, but do you really understand what's going on with her? Either she's having a bad day and taking it out on you, or something else besides the wait for her lunch order is bothering her. You don't know.

Understanding comes from listening closely and then, as in both of the preceding scenarios, taking the time to ask follow-up questions when needed. In the first scenario, if you followed up with the customer, you might learn that she asked a sales rep nine months ago to call her whenever a certain brand went on sale, and though the sales rep said she would make a note on the account, that didn't happen. Every time the customer comes in and sees that brand on sale, she gets angry that she wasn't called. In the second scenario, asking the customer questions helps you discover that the three minutes is really not what set her off; it was the fact that she told the counter rep who took her order that she was in a rush, to which he replied, "*Sorry. First come, first served.*" Now that you've dug deeper to understand the customers and the sources of the issues, you can address them.

In customer service, all constructive interactions come from trying to understand the perspective of the other person. Whether you're reacting to a customer complaint or proactively trying to personalize a customer's experience, making a good faith effort not only to listen to her but also to make sure you truly understand what she's trying to communicate and what she's failing to communicate is essential to having a successful interaction. The solution is as simple as listening carefully and asking questions, lots of questions.

CHAPTER 58

CATER to Your Customers with This Service Process

Let's take a look at a simple process you can apply to most customer service situations. If you've had any formal customer service training, you've likely been exposed to some version of this process. While the number of steps and the acronym might change from author to author, most people teaching reactive customer service use some combination of the following concepts. The CATER process we are about to discuss is the one I have found to be the most effective:

- *Concentrate* **on what the customer is saying.** We discussed the importance of listening and understanding in the previous chapter. Making sure you focus on the customer, so he knows you're paying attention to him and doing your best to understand his problem, is the start to working on any customer issue.
- *Acknowledge* **the customer's communication.** Acknowledge both the customer's feelings and the details of what she has said. This is often the best time to repeat information back to a customer. *"I understand how frustrating that must have been. I would be really upset if I showed up right when the clerk was closing the door and he wouldn't let me in."*
- *Thank* **and apologize.** Whenever you think it won't seem forced, thank the customer for bringing the matter to your attention, then deliver a sincere apology. Don't gush on about how sorry you are; just say, *"I apologize,"* or, *"I'm sorry,"* and include a quick reason why. (I believe "apologize" sends a much better message than "sorry" in most cases.) *"I want*

to thank you for bringing this to my attention. Our clocks don't automatically update, and it's possible they have gotten off. I also want to apologize for your experience. Our employee should never have just turned his back and pointed to the hours on the door."

- ***Explain* the reasons why.** Let the customer know why you aren't able to accommodate her request or, when appropriate, why something occurred. While there are certainly some things better left unsaid, when you can provide a reason why, it generally helps the customer be more understanding of the situation. The more valid your reason is in the customer's eyes, the more effective the technique. *"While he should never have communicated with you that way, I do want to let you know that we've begun enforcing a firm closing time due to security issues in the area and concern for the safety of our team. I just want to make sure we avoid disappointing you again in the future. Now, would it be okay if I . . ."*

- ***Resolve* the situation.** Do everything you can to solve the customer's problem or resolve her issue. When you can't directly give the customer what she's asking for, the key is to offer options, which we'll cover in more detail in the next chapter.

The CATER process is a simple and effective way to approach customer issues, but it's a guide, not a law. Service interactions in the real world won't always allow you the luxury of following a sequential process. In addition, you won't do every part of the process every time. Sometimes you won't apologize. Sometimes you won't explain why. And sometimes, no matter how hard you try, you won't be able to resolve. However, if you keep this process in mind as you work with customer issues, you'll find that it provides you a useful framework for addressing difficult service issues and for helping you avoid getting stuck wondering, "What do I do next?" As we proceed with the remainder of this book, you'll see this foundational process referred to occasionally as we build on it when addressing specific challenges.

CHAPTER 59

Focus on What You Can Do,
Not on What You Can't

Pivoting, which we discussed in Chapter 55, is about shifting a conversation from a place that's unproductive to one that's productive. Yet sometimes it's not the customer who needs to be moved onto productive ground, it's the service rep. All too often, customers want to focus on what's wrong, on what it is they want, and on why the rep can't give it to them. And all too often, service reps stay right there with them, focusing on what they can't do and never even telling the customer what they can do. One of the most valuable shifts in approach that customer-facing professionals can internalize is learning to focus on what they can do for the customer in any given situation.

In the beginning of an interaction, when you're unable to provide the customer with what she's asking for, you'll need to focus briefly on the "can't" part of the conversation. There's a good way to do this so you set the stage to move the conversation forward quickly. The most fundamental principle in telling a customer no is this: Don't use the word "no." People have a programmed response to it, and it's not a positive one. As children, when we wanted something and were told we couldn't have it, we were usually told no. We didn't like it then, and we don't like it now. When you have to tell a customer you're unable to accommodate her request, begin by dealing with the "can't" part of the conversation directly (*explain*), and then shift the conversation to what you can do (*resolve*). Sadly, too many frontline reps stop with explaining what they can't do.

One of the most obvious markers I have to spot frontline reps who need significant coaching on communicating with customers is when I hear them give "can't" answers that aren't followed up by alternatives or options. They tell customers what they can't do, then leave it at that:

- *"Sorry, we don't sell those here."* (Silence.)
- *"No, I can't. They don't allow us to go into the warehouse."* (Silence.)
- *"I'm not given the delivery schedule."* (Silence.)

The problem with dead-end answers is that they create dead-end experiences. You never want to present a customer with a closed-ended statement, particularly one that tells him you're unable to provide what he's asking for. If you aren't able to give the customer a positive response to his request, then come back with options of what you can do. This is the same concept that we discussed in Chapter 39, when we discussed acting as the customer's personal detective. In that chapter, we said that a Hero-Class rep never comes back empty-handed. The principle here is the same, except in this context it extends past trying to hunt down missing items or answer technical questions to virtually every interaction with a customer where you're unable to provide what he's looking for. From a request to waive a shipping charge to a major blowup over a missed delivery, the Hero-Class rep comes back with what he *can* do and tries to steer the conversation there.

Customers want what they want, and in the absence of getting what they want, they want answers and alternatives. If you're unable to give exactly what they want, then your focus needs to be on offering them the best possible options in the circumstances. Let's say a customer needs to know if the baby stroller she wants will be in the store by Thursday. You know you have three on order from the distribution center, but you aren't able to tell from your system what day they will arrive.

"I wish I could tell you right now," you say to the customer, *"but we don't have access to the delivery schedule through our in-store system. I'm happy to call the distribution center for you*

when they open in the morning, and I can call you tomorrow as soon as I get a response. Can I —"

"I won't be available tomorrow, and I'm traveling all week after that." she says curtly.

"I really apologize that I don't have an answer for you today, but I'm committed to make sure we get you this stroller as fast as we can. If you like, I can leave a message for you tomorrow. Also, if you don't mind my asking, how long will you be out of town? If you'll be back pretty soon, I can make sure we set aside one of the strollers for you so it's here when you return. Would that work for you?"

Like any customer service situation, there were many ways you could have gone. Depending on the customer's reactions, you could have offered to give her the inventory number to check it online or to email her the information. Assuming that it's reasonable, what you offer to do for the customer is generally less important than the fact that you offered something at all. Whether it's an alternative solution or simply an offer of information, let the customer know what you can do. You'll find that focusing on the "can" instead of the "can't" is often the difference between settling the customer down and making her more frustrated.

CHAPTER 60

Making It Right Is More Important Than Being Right

Far too many frontline reps approach disagreements with customers as battles to be won. They come at the customer like a prosecuting attorney, wanting to prove they're right more than anything. Pride is allowed to overtake service, defensiveness to ride roughshod over accommodation. The service interaction is allowed to devolve into an argument, and when that happens, the rep has already lost.

"*But what if I am right?*" frontline reps will often ask.

"So what?" I'll reply. "In 99 percent of cases, does it really matter?"

In most cases, it doesn't, and this is where our natural inclinations run counter to our ability to deliver a Hero-Class customer experience. Deep down, we want the customer to know he's wrong. We want to hold the moral high ground. We want him to know that we won't be played for a fool. We want him to know that we didn't screw up. We want him to know that he won't be rewarded for his lies and misrepresentations. But most of the time we're trying to send a message to those who aren't willing or able to receive it. Bestselling author Seth Godin summed the matter up succinctly in a blog post he published in May 2013 called "On teaching people a lesson":

> You're actually not teaching them a lesson, because the people who most need to learn a lesson haven't, and won't. What you're actually doing is diverting yourself from your path as well as ruining your day in a quixotic quest for fairness, fairness you're unlikely to find. [1]

The principle is very much the same for attempting to prevail in a dialogue with a customer. Whether you're simply trying to show that you're right or trying to show that you won't allow the person's anger, lies, or manipulation to be rewarded, you're most likely not "teaching" anyone a lesson; you're only diverting precious energy to satisfy some internal desire to "win." I get it; sometimes you don't want to give in. The customer is so blatantly wrong or is so obviously trying to take advantage of you that you don't want to give her the satisfaction. But in most cases, it's a fool's errand.

Now, none of what I've said so far should be taken to mean that the facts aren't important. Before I go into any call with an upset customer, I want to know the facts. I want to know what the client says we did or didn't do, and if that's true. It gives me a perspective on any operational issues that might be occurring and also gives me a glimpse into the customer himself. Was there a communication issue? Did he misunderstand something? Is he completely disconnected from reality? Understanding the facts can often yield important insights, but in most cases, I won't actually use the information with the customer, because proving that we're right and he's wrong is not my objective.

In addition to the insights the facts of a situation provide, there are a few specific circumstances in which I'll use this information to counter a customer with facts that contradict his assertion. The three scenarios are:

1. When the customer's misperception of the facts is making progress impossible. When other, less confrontational techniques have failed, sometimes it's necessary to address the facts head on to enable forward progress to be achieved. Let's say a customer keeps insisting that no one from your organization called to let him know his special order had arrived. *"Sir, I've just checked our records, and it shows we actually did call you three times. John left you a message on May 28, Stacy left you a message on May 30, and I person-*

ally left you a message yesterday. Perhaps we don't have the best number for you." In a situation like this, the facts can be useful to help a customer move on to a solution. When the customer fixates on what he perceives your organization did or did not do and refuses to allow you to move the conversation forward in a gentler manner, sometimes pushing back with the facts can help reset the conversation.

2. When you think establishing the customer's perception of the company's competence is important to long-term service. Sometimes you won't want the customer to walk away from the discussion believing her own misperceptions about what the company did or didn't do. You know that her belief, if not addressed, will solidify in her mind, that it'll become the frame through which she views future interactions. You want to either let the customer know that you did it correctly or, if you made a mistake, to help her understand that it's not how you usually do business.

3. When the customer's assertion has safety or liability implications. Occasionally a customer will make inaccurate claims that have liability implications. You know he's either mistaken or making it up. In situations like this, countering with the facts is usually important. Of course, following your company's policies and procedures when it comes to these types of claims is essential, but this is one of those situations where facts often need to be deployed to counter a customer's inaccurate assertions.

When choosing to counter a customer factually, deftness of touch is important. You want to counter in a way that does not escalate the situation but rather helps defuse it. More important, countering customers with facts should only be done when necessary, as in the above exceptions. Your goal is to work with the customer to resolve her issue and give her a great experience, even when her dissatisfaction might be based on some misunderstandings on her part. In the final analysis, you should never go into a client issue looking to be right, but only looking to make it right.

Notes

1. Seth Godin, "On Teaching People a Lesson," May 2013, http://seth godin.typepad.com/seths_blog/2013/05/on-teaching-people-a-lesson.html. Accessed September 23, 2014.

CHAPTER **61**

Let Upset Customers Punch
Themselves Out

One of the most powerful pieces of customer service advice I can give you for dealing with irritated, upset, or even angry customers is also one of the most simple: Let them punch themselves out. Punching oneself out is a phrase taken primarily from boxing but is used in many martial arts. It refers to when a fighter punches an opponent until he can't punch anymore. The fighter spends all of his energy, doesn't put his opponent away, and as a result has nothing left in the "tank" to attack further.

An upset customer can be remarkably similar. When he comes at you, he's usually full of energy and ready for battle. He has something he needs to get off his chest, and you're going to be the one to listen to it. Of course, being on the other end of the punches is no fun, but the good news is that if you let him go long enough, he'll eventually punch himself out, and you'll be ready for a conversation. (Obviously, I'm referring to punches metaphorically. The customer should not actually be punching you.) Now, the boxing metaphor goes only so far. Clearly, your goal is not to tire the customer out so you can punch back, but to let the customer tire himself out so he stops punching you.

Before we look at the details of using this technique, let's look at what happens when you don't use it. If you're like most reps, you respond defensively. You start to offer excuses, correct the customer, and in general try to explain the company's side of the situation. If you've had any customer service training, then you still jump in way too quickly, but at least you follow some sort of basic process of acknowledging, apologizing, and solving. It's a reflexive response. When you're getting lit up by a customer, you want to end it. You certainly don't want to sit there and let it continue, but in general, that's exactly what you should do. In fact, the angrier the customer is, the more you want to let her punch herself out.

I remember doing a training session with the customer experience supervisor at one of my retail businesses. I told her, "If you don't remember anything else from this training, just remember this: Let them punch themselves out. You're going to get the hard ones, and they'll be pretty upset by the time they get to you, so let 'em go off if they need to." When I asked her years later what one piece of advice had been most important to her in her job, she said it was letting customers punch themselves out.

Here's the basic three-step process:

1. Let them go. Let the customer say what she has to say for as long as she needs to say it. Now, this doesn't mean you should be completely silent. Listen for pauses or key points and use active listening to let her know you're engaged and listening to what she's saying, particularly if you're speaking with her on the phone.

2. Keep it going. When you think the customer is done or slowing down, wait for a good time and then ask her another open-ended question. Try to focus in on what you think she's really most upset about. *"I understand how frustrating the entire situation is. I noticed that you mentioned how the agent on the phone treated you. Can you tell me more about that?"* Most of the time, the customer isn't done after the first round. Give her permission to keep going. Usually, you'll get another earful.

3. Work the solution. Once she slows down or stops again (unless you feel she still has more left), that's the time to follow the CATER process we discussed in Chapter 58. Then ask questions as needed, either to clarify details or to find out what you can do to resolve the situation in a manner that will make her a happy customer again. A good rule of thumb is this: The longer and more intensely the customer has spoken, the more time you should spend empathizing, apologizing, and even explaining the company's side of the situation when appropriate. You want to connect with her about her situation so she knows that you truly understand how upset she is. In other words, don't let a customer go off for 15 minutes and then go straight into saying, "So what can I do to resolve this issue for you?" Once she's invested all that energy into venting to you, she's just as concerned with understanding that she was heard and that you know how she feels as she is with solutions.

One of the questions frontline reps often ask when discussing this technique is, *"What if I don't have time?"* This is a legitimate concern; some upset customers have a lot to say and can take a nice chunk out of your day saying it. In the end, it's a question of triage. Which approach creates the most benefit in the situation? If the effect of letting a customer punch herself out is to ignore customers who are expecting attention at that moment, then generally you might want to use an abbreviated version of the technique or avoid it altogether. If you simply have a lot on your to-do list (and who doesn't?), then you're often better served taking the time letting the customer punch herself out. If she has that much to say, doing what you can to reconcile the situation in the moment is likely to save you and the company more time and stress in the long run.

You should be aware when using this technique that in a small percentage of situations, it can backfire. On occasion, the process of speaking about the situation will make the customer angrier, especially if the situation has been going on for some time. The act of rehashing each detail will actually make the customer remember and relive all of the issues that got him to this point, and he'll get madder as he speaks. When this happens, it can generally resolve in one of two ways, and you'll have to make a judgment call to decide which way it's headed. Either he'll get angrier for part of the conversation but will eventually peak and start punching himself out, or he'll work himself into an increasingly angrier state. The latter situation should be avoided at all costs. The only way to know when this is happening is to pay close attention to the customer's tone, what he's saying, and the trajectory of his attitude. There's no hard-and-fast rule for which way to take the conversation. You simply need to be aware that the technique can backfire and to be actively looking for a customer who's working himself up more by talking.

In the end, letting upset customers punch themselves out works the vast majority of the time and is quite frankly one of the most powerful techniques for handling an angry customer that I've come across. Try it on your next few really upset customers; you'll be surprised how much easier to work with they become once they've punched themselves out.

CHAPTER 62

What to Do When the Customer Won't Stop Talking

On occasion, you may find yourself faced with a customer who won't stop talking. It can be because she wants to explain details she thinks you need in order to understand her situation. Or it can be that she wants to take you through everything that has happened with your company up to the present moment. It can even be because, as we saw in Chapter 61, she's upset about what happened and needs to vent. No matter what the larger context, there will often be occasions when you'll need to address the fact that a customer won't stop talking.

I purposely placed this chapter after our discussion of letting customers punch themselves out so I could address the fact that the two approaches are not contradictory. There's a time and place for letting customers talk themselves out and a time and place for, dare I say it, interrupting them. You have to know when each approach is warranted.

One of the most important times to consider interjecting is when you know you'll have to transfer the customer to someone else to resolve his issue. If you know early in the conversation that you're going to have to transfer the customer, then you don't want to let him tell you his whole story for five minutes. You have two choices: Let him go on or interrupt him. Both choices have pros and cons, and deciding between them requires judgment about what will be best received by the customer. For example:

"Excuse me, Sir. Forgive me for interrupting, but I want to be respectful of your time. I can tell from the information you've given me that I'll need to connect

you with someone else to assist you with your issue. I know how frustrating it can be to have to repeat your story to multiple people, so if I could just ask you a few specific questions, I should be able to connect you with someone who can help you."

If the moment is timed correctly and handled well, often an interjection such as this will be appreciated. Included in the language above are two components you want to make sure your interjection contains:

1. Acknowledge the interruption at the beginning. Although you should never talk over the customer, when you jump into a narrow pause, it's still an interruption. Both you and the customer know she wasn't finished speaking, so acknowledge it openly and professionally. *"Excuse me." "Forgive me for interrupting." "I apologize for jumping in."*

2. Make your interjection about the customer. The only reason to ever interrupt a customer is when doing so is to her benefit. So make sure to state why you did it immediately after you apologize. *"I'm sorry, but I can already tell that I'm going to have to connect you with another department. If you don't mind, please let me clarify a few details so I can get you to the correct place and you'll only have to tell your story once."*

Interrupting a customer is tricky business and should be handled with care. You won't always know if or when the time is right, but there will certainly be situations where interrupting is preferable to letting her tell her story for no reason. When those times occur, the tips above should make the process as smooth as possible.

CHAPTER 63

The Art of Framing

When the only options you have are less than what the customer wants, one of the most powerful approaches you can take is to frame the issue in a way that makes the solution most acceptable to the customer. Framing is a technique from psychology that involves presenting information in a positive (or negative) context in order to alter the impact it has on an individual or group; it's the careful use of words that makes people more likely to be receptive to a particular message.

To understand the concept of framing, let's look at a few quick examples in and out of a business setting:

- What would make you feel happier: if your best friend got a better job than you or if your best friend finally achieved her lifelong goal?
- Which deal would make you feel better: 20 percent off because you are valued as a customer or 20 percent off because room is needed for the new models?
- What would you choose: beef that is 75 percent lean or beef that is 25 percent fat?

If you answered that you prefer 75 percent lean beef, you're not alone. This is a framing choice that was presented in an actual experiment where participants rated the 75 percent lean beef as "being leaner, of higher quality, and less greasy."[1] The math is the same, of course, but the simple shift in framing significantly changed people's perceptions. I bet you're already seeing how this can be useful in customer service, so let's delve into a few examples of how you might use framing to make conversations with customers more effective:

- If you want to create a better reception for a delay, you could say, "*I can have the part for you as early as Tuesday,*" rather than, "*I can't get you the part until Tuesday.*"
- If you want to help make a tough answer go down easier, you could say, "*The chef is willing to create a personalized special just for you,*" rather than, "*Unfortunately, we're sold out of the special.*"
- If you need customers to understand the benefits of what you are offering, you could say, "*This model actually does what you're looking for more efficiently,*" rather than, "*This model is the closest thing we have to the one you want.*"

Framing works even better when combined with other psychological concepts that affect customer behavior. For instance, customers are loss averse; they'd rather not lose than gain. "*I want to make sure you don't lose all of the points you have worked so hard to accumulate by leaving our program.*" A different approach can be to use an unattractive third option to influence a customer's choice. Let's say a customer wanted a cash refund, which you're not authorized to give. You could frame it in such a way that the cash refund was the least attractive option. "*I can put the refund on a store credit or store gift card right now, or I can submit a request to my manager for a cash or check refund, but that could take up to a week.*"

A simple word can affect a customer's frame. One experiment asked observers of a car wreck how fast one of the cars was going. One group was asked about the speed when the cars "crashed" while another group was asked about the speed when the cars "contacted."[2] The "crashed" group, viewing the same wreck, estimated the speeds higher than the "contacted" group. Similarly, you can be on the lookout for what the customer cares about and use words that support these feelings to frame your response. If a customer seems focused on price or getting a deal, use terms like *"best value"* or *"biggest discount."* If a customer seems upset about being ignored, use terms like *"the attention you deserve"* and *"how much we value you as a customer."* The power words listed in Chapter 51 can be very effective here.

Framing's usefulness is not limited to reactive situations like the ones listed in this chapter. It can be used in your emails, in your scripts, and in your signage. However, it's important to note that framing is not always universal. As with anything having to do with language, it can impact different social groups differently. Framing is also most effective when done subtly, without forcing any of the techniques to the point where they seem awkward.

Framing helps your customers see the world the way you hope they'll see it. Whether you choose to employ it as a technique or not, you should be aware that you're framing all the time. No matter what you say, it's creating a frame in which the customer is going to interpret your words. You can either control what that frame looks like or you can leave it to chance. As long as what you're saying is truthful and gives the customer the information she needs, why would you consider using language that is less effective at communicating your intent and creating a framework for a more positive customer experience?

Notes

1. Craig McKenzie and Jonathan Nelson, "What a Speaker's Choice of Frame Reveals: Reference Points, Frame Selection, and Framing Effects," *Psychonomic Bulletin and Review* 10, no. 3 (2003), 596, http://psy2.ucsd.edu/~mckenzie/McKenzie&NelsonPBR2003.pdf. Accessed September 23, 2014.

2. Noam Shpancer. "Framing: Your Most Important and Least Recognized Daily Ment," *Psychology Today,* December 22, 2010, http://www.psychologytoday.com/blog/insight-therapy/201012/framing-your-most-important-and-least-recognized-daily-ment. Accessed September 23, 2014.

CHAPTER **64**

Sales Techniques That Help Close the Deal

As we discussed in Chapter 48, techniques that are primarily associated with the discipline of sales can be very effective when applied to customer service. It helps to think of the word sales broadly. In a general sense, you're always selling something. For example, if there's a difference between what the customer wants and what you can provide, you're selling him on a solution. It stands to reason, then, that if selling is part of customer service, some of the techniques that are effective in the sales process might also be useful to customer-facing reps. So let's take a look at two sales techniques that are extremely effective in customer service: asking closing questions and isolating the objection.

Closing techniques are tactics that are designed to close the sale, to reach agreement and finalize the discussion. They're intended to end stalling on the part of the customer and to either make the sale or discover what objections the customer has. In customer service, the use of closing questions accomplishes essentially the same purpose: to get agreement on a resolution of the issue or determine that you're not there yet and need to understand better what the customer wants.

Here are some closing techniques and how to approach them:

- **Concession Close.** Here you are offering the customer a concession and asking if that will satisfy her. You can generally use some version of the following: *"If I could _____ , would that _____?"* *"If I could apply a credit for the difference to your account, would that work for you?"*

- **Trial Close.** Trial closes are small closes you use along the way that lead to the final close. In larger sales processes, the salesperson is looking to get a certain number of "yes" answers to get him to the final "yes." In customer service, you're testing the waters to see if you're heading in the right direction. *"If I could ship the dress to you on your trip, is that something you would be interested in?"* Or you can ask more general questions. *"Are we heading in the right direction?" "How is this sounding so far?"*

- **Choice Close.** Sometimes in a challenging customer service situation, the customer wants Solution A, but all you have is Solution B or C. When these conversations stall out and continue to go in circles, the "choice close" can help you force a decision. *"I apologize, Ma'am, but we simply aren't able to do that. Would you prefer ____ or ____?"*

- **Directive Close.** This technique involves taking an assumptive approach with the customer. You're assuming she is ready to be closed and using language that directs her toward your desired end result. *"The next step is for me request the return authorization. Would you like me to email you the number or give you a call?"* Only use this closing technique if you're in a positive place with the customer but can't seem to get her to make a decision. Do not use this technique if the customer is upset at all, as it will seem pushy.

- **Ultimatum Close.** This technique is an absolute last resort for when you're simply stuck, have tried multiple options, and the customer will simply not be satisfied. You've decided that it's time to move on, one way or another, so you give the customer an ultimatum. *"Sir, I'm really at the limits of what I can offer. Is the option I presented acceptable to you?"* If the customer says no, my favorite line to follow up with is, *"I wish I could do more, but that's as far as I can go. How would you like to proceed from here?"*

Another powerful technique from sales is isolating the objection; in our case, it's isolating the solution. In sales, the goal is to remove all other objections by getting the customer to agree that he has only one objection remaining. This is done using the framework, *"If I can (handle the objection), then will you (close the deal)?"* *"So Mr. Jones, let me ask you: Your real concern is the length of the warranty, correct? So if I can make this warranty work for you, are you ready to buy today?"* If he agrees, then the salesperson simply has one objection to contend with, and she makes the sale.

In customer service, this works when you have a customer who can't seem to stick to one issue. Of course, many customer service issues are multidimensional, but you've been working with him awhile and have used all the standard processes and language. Yet it seems that every time you get close to a solution, he brings up another minor detail or goes back to ground you thought you'd already covered. If you feel you've done all you can to acknowledge him and understand his concerns, then you should be at a point where you can focus the conversation by isolating the objection. *"Sir, I know your time is valuable, and I want to help lock down a solution that will make you happy. I've already reversed the credit card charge; now, I want to focus on getting you a trainer that you'll love while Beth is out on maternity leave. If I can help schedule you with the right trainer, will that work for you?"*

As you can see, these two techniques can be extremely powerful when applied to the right situations. No technique is a match for every scenario, however, and it's important to pay close attention to the situation and the customer's state of mind before using either of them. Context is everything. But if you can learn to read the customer and to apply the right technique at the right time, you'll find these approaches can help resolve your customer interactions more efficiently and more effectively.

CHAPTER 65

Use Your Authority

If you're in a frontline position, you're probably wondering what this chapter is doing here. "What authority?" I can imagine you asking. Believe it or not, many frontline service reps have a lot more ability to use authority to impact customer perceptions than they think.

As a business owner, I understand the power of authority. When I have to address a customer service issue (and only the really tough ones make it to my desk), the first thing I say when I call the customer is "This is Adam Toporek. I'm the owner of CTS Service Solutions." Why? Because the owner is the ultimate authority. Sadly, customers are generally calmer and more respectful with me than they are with my staff. I know a lot of bosses don't understand this, but I think it's an important part of customer service to acknowledge: Customers will treat frontline staff with less respect than they will treat a manager or owner.

We've seen this first-hand in one of my retail operations. My wife, who ran the business, had numerous phone calls and encounters with customers yelling at or berating her. Oftentimes, when she was partway through a conversation, she would mention that she was "the owner" or "the wife of the owner," and the customer would do a complete 180. He'd get super nice and completely change his approach to the conversation. It was beyond pathetic, but it shows why you should use any authority you have to gain credibility with the customer.

Here are four personal attributes you can embrace to create perceived authority with customers:

- **Formal Title.** If you're not a full-blown manager, don't sweat it. Are you anything? A shift supervisor? The closing lead?

The head of rubber bands? If you've got it, flaunt it. *"Hi, Ma'am. I'm Sheila, and I'm the lead closer. I'd be happy to help you out."* Just saying a title, no matter what it is, can have an impact on a customer's perceptions.

- **Length of Service.** Believe it or not, this can really work. If you've been with the company for a while, use that. *"Hi, Ma'am. I'm Bill, and I've been with the company for three years. I've worked with a lot of customers with this same issue, and I'm sure I can help you."* People associate time at a company with authority. In most cases, if you've been there over a year, you can use it to create instant authority and credibility.
- **Specialized Training.** Have you had any specialized training, even not-so-specialized training that you can refer to? Don't lie or embellish, but don't be afraid to use what you've got. *"Hi, Sir. I've received the advance training on this system. I'm not sure if it can do what you are looking for, but if anybody can figure it out for you, I can."*
- **Specialized Expertise.** If you have specialized expertise, even if it is informal, you can use that as well. *"I can help you with that sir. I'm sort of the go-to gal around here for color matching. I'm actually in school for interior design."* Of course, if you use this tactic, be sure you really know what you're talking about, as the customer could very well know a lot about the topic also.

While using authority is particularly helpful when working with challenging customers or difficult situations, it can also be useful in simply answering questions or in making sales. Credibility is an important part of trust, and anything you can do to help customers understand your experience and expertise adds not only to your credibility but to the credibility of your organization. Think about some of the challenging situations you've been involved with or stepped into in the past few months, and then think about how you might have used your authority to make the situation go more smoothly.

CHAPTER **66**

Don't Blame the Policy for the Problem

Now that we've looked at techniques you can apply to difficult customer service situations, we're going to look at a few specific situations that frontline professionals often encounter and identify some specific approaches to handling them.

The first of these situations arises when a customer's desires are frustrated by your company's policies. When you talk about the phrases customers hate to hear, *"I'm sorry, it's our company policy"* has to be near the top of the list. The word "policy" is a problem in and of itself, but a bigger problem is the word "our," because to customers, if it's your policy you have the power to change it. Of course, the reality for most frontline reps is that you have policies you must abide by, and you'll rarely have the power to alter them.

When a customer's issue runs headlong into company policy, your best tactic is to avoid using it as an excuse. If mentioning the policy is necessary, then don't frame it as such. Simply explain why you're unable to accommodate the customer, and then suggest what you can do. If you're dealing with an issue completely outside of either your control or your company's control, such as something in violation of local, state, or federal regulations, you can lean on those a bit heavier. Customers are more understanding if the impediment is out of your company's control, as long as the next thing out of your mouth is what you can do for them. Regardless of whether the challenge is an internal policy or federal law, have options you can offer the customer. For instance, let's say a customer wants you to watch her children while she gets a tanning session, and it's your company policy that you can't watch children:

"I understand, Ma'am. I truly wish that I could watch them, but I'm unable to do so because I'll be unable to properly do my job. I often have to go to the back to check on the booths and clean the rooms, so your kids would be unsupervised. I'm sure you can understand. I know you said you wanted to get in before your friend's wedding tomorrow. Is there any way I can get you in later today, when you've had a chance to drop the kids off? I can give you a 20 percent discount for your inconvenience."

One way to prepare yourself for situations such as this is to know the typical policy challenges ahead of time and make sure you're aware of what, if anything, you can do to work around them. Perhaps in this case, in addition to offering appointment options and a discount, you could have offered a significant discount on the house brand of self-tanner. No matter what the policy or what the customer wants, avoid making company policy the reason you can't help the customer whenever possible. The situation will generally resolve quicker and easier if you take another tack.

CHAPTER 67

Fine Print Isn't Always So Fine for Customers

One of the worst ways a customer can learn that a company policy stands between her and what she wants is through fine print. Customers hate fine print, and they've all been in too many situations where it's been used to ensnare them or to try to pull a bait and switch. The first step in contending with issues involving fine print is to accept that it's necessary. In fact, in today's business environment, fine print is inevitable. The morass of legal and liability issues that modern organizations must navigate makes it a necessity. It may be a hassle, and it may seem like a bunch of gibberish from your company's legal department, but it's important gibberish that's designed to prevent much larger problems. If you can't understand the reasons for the fine print your organization uses, you're not going to be very convincing when discussing it with a customer, and doing so is crucial because customers can have intense reactions when they come into conflict with your company's fine print.

Sometimes the customer will be upset that he did not see the fine print and blame the company for burying such an important message. Of course, the company put the situation in fine print because it expected that less than 1 percent of customers would be affected by the issue. However, the customer will never see it that way. He's part of that 1 percent, and as far as he's concerned, everyone else is just like him. In this situation, you can empathize and agree (sort of). *"Sir, I certainly understand how this should have been called out more prominently in your case. I think our ad agency was not expecting it to be an issue, but I can see now how it affected you. How about if I . . . ."*

Other customers will consider any issue that arises from fine print as your company's attempt to take advantage of them. One approach to these customers is to flip the script. Let the customer know that the language is not there to take advantage of him but is actually there to prevent people from taking advantage of the company. *"I apologize, Sir. The language is there because we've had issues in the past. It's certainly not designed for loyal customers like you, and I'm really sorry it caused a problem for you in this case."*

No matter what type of organization you work for, chances are it uses fine print that, at some point, will upset a customer. Handling these fine-print situations will always be a delicate dance. You don't want to throw your company under the bus—*"Our lawyers make them put that on there"*—but you do want to empathize with the customer and explain the reasons why the fine print exists. If you can come to understand the necessity of fine print, you can use the approaches discussed in this chapter to get a Hero-Class result.

CHAPTER 68

Handling Customer Service "Experts"

Sometimes people who deal with customers in their jobs—supervisors, managers, business owners—can be among the worst customers. These self-appointed experts love to throw their experience or position around, and they usually do so to bully you. They want to show you that they know your job better than you do, even if they really don't have a clue. Perhaps you've heard comments like these before:

- *"If I treated my customers like you do, I'd be out of business in a week."*
- *"Don't they teach you anything about customer service here? I'm the customer; you're supposed to do what I want."*
- *"I run a sales team of 50 people, and if one of my people treated a customer like this, I'd fire them in ten seconds."*

When I first opened one of my retail stores, an upset customer sent repeated communications to tell me how bad our customer service was. We should be doing this, and we should be doing that, she continued to inform me. We *had* dropped the ball on a couple of occasions, but many of her demands were unrealistic. In one phone call, she suggested I hire her as a consultant to teach us "how to do customer service right." Somehow, though, I figured someone with unrealistic demands who resorted to threats and insults when she didn't get her way probably did not have much to teach my team about customer service.

In addition to following the standard processes you are learning in this book, these so-called experts require an extra-special approach: Feed their egos. *"Wow, Ma'am, it sounds like you really know a lot about customer service; I really appreciate your pointing out how we can do better."* Another approach is to solicit their advice, but in a way that you frame the issue. *"You seem to have a lot of expertise in this area, Sir. Can I ask you, what do you recommend someone in my position do in this situation when I don't have access to customer's information?"*

The key is understanding that these individuals will only respond in a productive fashion once you acknowledge their "superior" knowledge. If you recognize customer service "experts" as experts, you can begin to transition them to a solution they will be happy with.

CHAPTER 69

When a Complaint Is a Scam

In almost any frontline service position, you will, on occasion, have to contend with customers (or pretend customers) attempting to scam you and your company. It's an unavoidable part of doing business, and you need to be prepared to handle these situations firmly and professionally. Scamming is one of those topics where there can be a considerable philosophical difference of opinion on how such situations should be handled. One line of reasoning suggests that the damage from the scam is nowhere near as bad as the damage that may be done to your business if you anger the customer, and for this reason it's sometimes necessary to let the customer get away with the scam. In some cases, there's merit to this outlook, but in the majority of cases it's ridiculous. So let's briefly look at the mythology behind the give-customers-whatever-they-want-it-will-be-better-in-the-long-run philosophy, and then let's look at how you can address scam artists on your own service floor.

Have you ever heard the Nordstrom tire story? If you haven't, the short version is that many years ago, a gentleman walked into a Nordstrom store to return a set of tires. Nordstrom has never sold tires, but according to the story (the truth of which is in question), the Nordstrom rep was so empowered and customer focused that he or she refunded the tires, even though they were obviously not bought there.[1] The Nordstrom tire story has been a staple of trainers and customer service speakers for years. I've used this story myself. However, years ago I realized that for all the positive message the story carried, it also sent a message that was unrealistic and that frontline service professionals could not relate to. *"Return products that weren't even purchased here? I'm not even allowed to accept returns on the stuff we sell after 30 days!"* When I speak on the topic of customer service, I like to juxtapose the customer service fantasy world of the Nordstrom tire story with the reality of an actual modern Nordstrom policy.

Wardrobing, the act of buying a nice piece of clothing, wearing it once, and returning it, is an $8.8 billion problem for the retail industry. In order to combat this problem, Nordstrom has a visible tag sewn onto the outside of its special-occasion dresses. If the tag is not still in place when the dress is returned, Nordstrom can refuse to accept the return.[2] It may or may not do so based on the individual circumstances, but the point is that even Nordstrom has created a system so that it has the option to refuse returns based on wardrobing. That's customer service in the real world.

There are times when it makes sense to allow customers to get one over on you. This is particularly true when you're not absolutely certain they're scamming. Let's say your business sends out special coupons to its top loyalty-program members that are good for one visit. One of these members comes in and says she lost her coupon. You can see on the computer that her coupon for this promotion was already used. Is she lying? Did her daughter take her coupon and use it? You probably won't know, and the $10 discount is nothing compared to the business she gives the company. In this case, you would probably just let her have the discount.

In those situations where you're confronted with a customer who you think is trying to scam your company, I suggest asking yourself the following questions when determining how to handle it:

1. How serious is the scam?
2. Would letting the customer get away with it create a dangerous precedent?
3. Is the person a serial offender?
4. Is it outright stealing or simply taking advantage?

When you must stand up to a customer who is trying to scam your company, the most important thing to remember is to avoid accusing him of what he's really doing. You know what he's doing, and he knows you know, but it just lays there unsaid as you both play your parts. Your part is simply to follow the CATER process described in Chapter 58: Explain why you can't do what he wants and try to focus on what you can do as an alternative. If the customer is really trying to scam you, the interaction may not be that pleasant, but in the real world, you sometimes have to draw the line when someone insists he bought a set of tires from your cupcake store.

Notes

1. Snopes.com, "Return to Spender," April 2011, http://www.snopes.com/business/consumer/nordstrom.asp. Accessed September 23, 2014.

2. Cotten Timberlake and Renee Dudley, "Bloomingdale's Black Tags End Party for Next-Day Returns," Bloomberg, September 17, 2013, http://www.bloomberg.com/news/2013-09-17/bloomingdale-s-black-tags-end-party-for-next-day-returns.html. Accessed September 23, 2014.

CHAPTER **70**

Applying What You Know When the Heat Is On

In my experience working with frontline reps, I've found that no other topic is as important to them or resonates more with them than how to handle nightmare customers. While we like to use positively framed language, sometimes what's more important is dealing with reality head on. And I want you to know that I understand that whether we're talking about angry customers, mean customers, or just plain crazy customers, some customers are just nightmares. If you're like every frontline rep I've ever met, you want to be better prepared to handle these customers when you come across them. In fact, I feel certain a few readers will skip the beginning of this book and jump right to this part. That's okay, but it should be noted that this part of the book relies significantly on the parts that have come before it.

You've already learned much of what you need to know to handle nightmare customers. You'll need to work on your own mindset, as covered in Part One; to understand the customer's mindset, as covered in Parts Two and Three; to use great communication skills, as covered in Part Six; and to use techniques for challenging situations, as covered in Part Seven. In this part, we're going to lean heavily on the fact that you're already familiar with the tips and techniques previously covered in this book and simply look at a few additional tactics for when the customer heat is really on.

Whether you've skipped to this part or read the entire book up to this point, the important thing to bear in mind is that handling high-intensity customer service situations is not about single-shot techniques but about an entire repertoire of skills and tactics that are used together in the right order, in the right tone, and at the right time. And as you're about to discover, even then, it won't always work.

CHAPTER 71

There's No Silver Bullet for a Hand Grenade

I know how much frontline reps can dread nightmare customers. I can spend half a day talking about customer service to a roomful of frontline reps and can tell them how to succeed at 99 percent of their job, but when I open up the floor for questions, most of them will go straight to the 1 percent issues: "How do I handle a customer who is going off on me, who is completely irrational, and who is just plain crazy?" "How do I handle a customer who is foaming at the mouth, has flames shooting from his eyes, and has a voice like a Hollywood monster?"

Before I answer those questions in detail, I want to share a story with you that I like to tell frontline teams. It's about a new Army recruit who's learning to throw a hand grenade during basic training. At one point his instructor walks by and says, "Good throw, son."

The private thanks him and then says, "Sir, may I ask you a question?"

"Yes private."

"What do I do if someone throws a hand grenade at me?"

"Take cover," the sergeant replies.

"What if there is no cover?"

"Hit the deck."

"And what if that doesn't work?"

"It won't."

The private looks at the sergeant, eyes wide. "It won't?"

"No, but it's better than standing up."

I think I've had 100 different versions of this conversation with team members over the years. They come to me with the craziest situations imaginable, and ask, "What should I do?" So I tell them, "Do this," and if that doesn't work, "Do that." Inevitably, they'll ask, "But what if that doesn't work?"

My standard reply is, "You know what, it might not."

As I'm confronted with their empty stares, I can only imagine them thinking, "Thanks. A lot of good you are."

You see, before we embark on discussing nightmare customers, I have to be blunt with you: I don't have a silver bullet that will stop a hand grenade. I'll beg your forgiveness for the mixed metaphor, because I've found that it's a vivid visual to represent the idea that there's no single, magical technique that will work on every irate customer. When a customer explodes, it's going to be tough, it's going to be messy, and you're going to take some shrapnel. You can't fix stupid, crazy, or furious—you can only deal with them as best as you can.

Now for the good news. The absolute best way to avoid a hand grenade blast is to make sure no one ever throws one at you, and if you embrace Hero-Class customer service and use the techniques you have learned elsewhere in this book, you'll prevent a lot of service issues from ever escalating into nightmare scenarios. Additionally, if you use the tactics taught in this book, you'll be able to handle those situations better than 99 percent of frontline reps. Far too many service reps get their backs up once a customer starts yelling at them; their reaction to a hand grenade landing at their feet is to throw a box of dynamite on top of it. Yet most angry customers can be turned around. You can defuse your customers' anger, and with the right approach, you can even make them happy. While you won't win them all, every situation can be handled in a way that makes it better and not worse. So now let's look at how you can do just that.

CHAPTER 72

13 Go-To Tactics for Defusing Angry Customers

Few people enjoy working with angry or irate customers. It's unpleasant, unfulfilling, and sometimes unmanageable. One of the reasons working with these customers is so difficult is that anger is a natural trigger for most people. We react to it in specific ways, and none of those ways are useful in customer service. In this chapter, we're going to look at specific tactics for handling angry customers. As I mentioned in Chapter 71, none of the techniques are silver bullets; when you deal with an angry customer, you can expect to take some licks, but used calmly and wisely, they can help you succeed in situations where the great majority of service reps fail.

Let's get started with a few tactics that will help you maintain a productive mindset when faced with an angry customer:

1. Don't get emotional. As hard as it can be, detach yourself from the emotions of the moment. Remember that it's just a job; it's not personal. More important, remember that you are not responsible for how your customer feels.

2. Don't take the bait. Customers will try to draw you into an argument. Don't take the bait, because once you do, the customer owns you. You've stooped to his level and have acted emotionally and unprofessionally. In addition, he also now knows that he can get a reaction from you and will continue to try to push your buttons.

3. Don't accept the customer's frame. Often, the customer will try to trap you with comments that are framed with a built-in accusation. *"If you cared about customer privacy, you'd be able to find my records."* Do not accept the customer's frame. *"We have some of the highest privacy standards in the industry, and we take privacy very seriously. Because we made a mistake does not mean that we don't care."*

Now let's move on to some tactics that will help you communicate in the most effective way possible in these situations:

4. Use soft language and a calm tone. Don't add fuel to the fire by matching the customer's emotional intensity. You want to use a calm, even tone that helps de-escalate the situation.

5. Don't tell the customer to calm down. One of the worst things you can do is to tell someone who is amped up to "calm down" or to "relax." It will come across both as a criticism of the person's emotional state and as you bossing her around.

6. Do not crowd the customer's space. If you're interacting with an angry customer in person, don't violate the customer's personal space. Keep a healthy distance, and beware of the tendency to try to lower the customer's volume by moving closer to him.

7. Maintain neutral hands. Keep your hands calmly at your sides. Avoid strong gestures while speaking, and, of course, do not point at the customer or fold your arms.

8. Maintain a neutral face. Many people are unaware of how much they display what they are thinking through their facial expressions. Be aware of your expression and make sure it conveys concern and attentiveness, not emotion.

9. Be respectful. Angry customers will often treat you without respect. You want to rise above that behavior and treat them with the utmost respect. Use terms of courtesy and respect throughout the encounter.

10. Replace "but" with "and." We're all used to saying things like, "*I really want to help you, but my hands are tied.*" Since we're used to saying it, we're also used to hearing it, and the word "but" instantly tells us that we are being rejected. When possible, try to substitute "and" for "but" in these situations. Compare the sentence, "*I really want to refund your money right now, but I don't have manager access,*" with, "*I really want to refund your money right now, and if my manager were here with the code, I would do it this instant.*" The only time you really want to use a "but" statement is when you are intentionally making a strong point with a customer.

Finally, let's end with a few tactics you can use when nothing else seems to be working:

11. Try to move the customer to a more private area. Sometimes when a customer is really upset, it helps to move him to a less public area. It's more pleasant for the other customers, and often the angry customer is not happy about sharing his details publicly. Use your judgment in these cases (and, of course, follow your company's policies) to determine if you can move to a more private area and if you need to have a witness present. Also be mindful of safety concerns when making these decisions. However, when the circumstances are right, you will find moving to a more private area can often help de-escalate a situation.

12. Allow the customer to cool off. Often, a customer just needs to calm down. Anger is not just a mental response but also a chemical response, and it takes time for the mind to settle down. Obviously, you won't always have the ability to disengage and allow someone to calm down, but if you can, sometimes it is the best option. Once you realize nothing will be accomplished if the customer doesn't settle down—and it looks like that's not going to happen—you might be better off if you disengage temporarily. We'll discuss this topic in more detail in Chapter 73.

13. Replace the face. If you think a customer has latched onto *you* as the problem, you're probably better off bringing in a fresh face, one that the customer's anger is not directed toward. Most of the time, these situations are not about you, but when you become one of the sources of the customer's anger, it's time to transition to a new face. *"Sir, it's apparent that I'm unable to assist you in the way you need me to. I think the best way for me to help you is to let you work with Laura. Do you mind if I go get her?"* No matter how you tailor your approach to the specific situation, you generally want to begin by *asking* to bring in someone new and then, if the customer won't go along with the soft approach, by *telling* him you'll be having him work with someone else.

Angry customers, irate customers, or nightmare customers— one reason they're all so difficult for customer-facing reps to handle is because people who end up in customer service–related positions are generally pretty nice; they want to make customers happy. Working your way through these tough situations begins and ends with controlling your natural reactions and depersonalizing the interaction. Once you do that, you can use the techniques in this chapter strategically and effectively to succeed in situations where most frontline reps fail.

CHAPTER 73

How to Draw the Line with a Customer

In Chapter 1, I stated that you and the customer are not on equal terms. In Chapter 4, I said it's your job to take crap from the customer. However, there are limits—always. Sometimes customers are so unreasonable, so unwilling to be satisfied, and so abusive that you have the right to end the conversation. When a customer crosses the line from anger to abuse, the only practical option may be to disengage from the situation.

What is abuse? Truly, it's in the eye of the beholder, but here are a few examples:

- Unwavering insistence on unrealistic demands that the customer knows, or should know, are not remotely appropriate to the situation
- Verbal harassment of the customer service rep with inappropriate language
- Repeated threatening of adverse actions if the customer does not get what he wants (e.g., blackmail)

Of course, the gamut of abusive behavior is much wider than this, but the list above gives a sense of what is meant by the term. How you react to abuse depends on whether you feel the customer was truly being abusive or had a momentary "losing of the cool" that she could walk back from. You'll have to be the judge. If you do feel the need to disengage from a customer who has become abusive, here are a few phrases you can use to warn a customer that you're going to end the conversation or to actually do so:

- *"Sir, if you continue to talk to me like that, I'm going to have to end this conversation."*
- *"Ma'am, if you continue to use that language, I'm going to have to end this call."*
- *"Sir, I would really like to help you, but if you can't refrain from personally attacking me and using foul language, I'll have to end this conversation."* (These situations are one of the few times I recommend using a "but" statement with a customer.)

In such situations, when you're simply warning the customer that if he continues to be abusive you'll end the conversation, the next step is to quickly follow up each warning with a solution-focused question. *"Now, do you mind if I ask you about what you said was wrong with the replacement item?"*

If you must terminate the conversation, simply tell the customer that you're doing so in a professional but firm manner. If the customer is in a store, you might do so by referring to your manager, as you don't want to just leave him sitting there with access to other customers or colleagues:

- *"Sir, I told you that I would not continue this conversation if you continued to speak to me like that. I'm going to get my manager, and you're welcome to wait here if you would like to speak with her."*
- *"Ma'am, I told you that I would not continue this conversation if you continued to use that language. I'm disconnecting the call now. Please feel free to call back when we can have a professional discussion, and I'll be glad to try to assist you."*

When a customer becomes abusive, you should always understand that you have the right to disconnect from such situations, and you should do so calmly and professionally. The line between anger and abuse will be different for each person, but just because you're expected to have a thick skin when working with customers doesn't mean you should have to put up with being personally abused. There's a line even the customer should not be allowed to cross; don't be afraid to point it out if you have to.

CHAPTER **74**

How to Handle Customer Threats

One of the sad realities of customer service is that a small percentage of customers will resort to threats to attempt to get what they want. Reasons vary. Perhaps the customer is exasperated and is lashing out. Perhaps the customer hasn't gotten what she wants and is escalating it to see if you will back down. Perhaps the customer is just not a very nice person and likes to threaten people. Once someone threatens you, it changes the dynamic of the conversation; in fact, depending on the severity of the threat, it might actually end the conversation.

In this chapter, we're going to walk through some typical threats you will face on the front lines of customer service and give you some helpful hints for addressing these situations. My goal is not just to show you how to address these threats but also to put these threats in perspective. I want you to see that most threats you receive in customer service really aren't that threatening.

- **"I'm going to take my business down the street."** This threat amounts to nothing more than stating the obvious, as this is the implied threat in every customer service encounter. When a customer voices it, it's because the customer is not getting what she wants from the conversation and has resorted to actually saying what you both already know: Unless stuck due to contractual or switching barriers, unhappy customers tend to go elsewhere. Two good options for addressing this threat are:
  - **Ignore it.** If you think the threat was just mentioned as part of a larger offloading of feelings, then simply don't go there. If the customer's primary focus was not the

threat, and it was just something said in anger, then focus on problem solving and moving forward.

- **Pivot it.** In this case, you simply want to acknowledge the feelings behind the threat and pivot to how you're going to do everything you can to make the customer not want to go through with it. *"I understand, Sir, truly. If I felt the way you do, I would take my business down the street too, but my goal today is to do everything I can to make sure not only that you stay with us but that when you walk out this door you're looking forward to coming back to see us. Now, if you don't mind, can I ask you a question?"*

• **"I'm going to bash you online / I'm going to report you to the Better Business Bureau."** These two threats are first cousins and are probably the most common leveled at businesses nowadays. Consumers are drunk with the power of the Internet and social media, and they vastly overestimate its power in the case of a simple customer service disagreement.

During the financial crisis of 2008, the Better Business Bureau (BBB) complaints for one of my retail stores spiked. It was still just a handful, but the cases had no merit and were based on people trying to bully us into refunds to which they were not entitled. I asked the BBB representative in our area if it had seen an increase in complaints since the crash, and she told me they had more than doubled. "You didn't hear it from me," she said, "but people are using us to try to get money back."

You see, making good on BBB threats is relatively easy and costs nothing but time; making good on online threats costs nothing in money and takes even less time. Yet, like many things in life, the more rare something is, the more valuable it is, and online comments might be one of the least rare things on earth. Online comments about companies are a dime a dozen, and while you should be concerned about *every* online comment, you should take care not to allow customers to bully you with threats of negative online reviews (we will discuss this further in Chapter 79). Of course, this assumes that neither you nor your company has actually done something horribly bad or embarrassing, or you're not being threatened by someone with 10 million Twitter followers. Use your judgment when evaluating the threat.

One of my favorite recommendations for dealing with a customer who threatens to "rip you a new one on Facebook" is simply to ask him one of the following questions:

- *"What do you hope to accomplish by going online?"*
- *"If you wrote something online, what would you say?"*

Your reply to whatever his answer might be is then fairly simple: *"My goal is to help you accomplish that right now. I want to help you fix every one of those challenges so that when you leave here today, the only thing you have left to write about is how much you love it here. I'd really appreciate one more chance to make that happen for you."*

- **"I'm going to report you to the manager."** This threat is often used to push around frontline reps and others who have layers above them in the business hierarchy. The customer has decided that threatening the livelihood of the person in front of her by potentially getting him "in trouble" is the way to get what she wants. There are many variations on this theme. For instance, in franchises or chains, customers will often threaten owners or managers with reporting them to the corporate office. Here are two approaches for this situation:
  - **Don the cloak of failure.** You essentially want to take the approach that if the customer is asking for a manager, you have failed her. This form of agreement is very unusual—the customer is expecting you to feel threatened—and she will often change her approach. *"Ma'am, I'm really sorry to hear you say that, not because I'm worried about getting in trouble, but*

because I know that if you feel that way, then I've failed to make you happy. And making you happy is my goal. I'd love it if you could just give me another chance to see what I can do to turn this around for you."

– **Become the customer's transition partner.** Sometimes it's obvious you're not going to be able to help the customer. In those cases, use the threat as an opportunity to help transfer her to where she might be able to get her issue resolved. *"You know Ma'am, at this point, I think that's a good idea. It's obvious that I'm unable to resolve your issue, and I'm truly sorry for that. If you'll let me, I'd like to personally make sure you get to my manager so she can help resolve this issue positively for you."*

• **"My brother-in-law works for WBS-TV."** This is a version of the online threat on steroids. The customer hopes to scare you into thinking that with one phone call, the I-Team investigators will have you and your shady practices plastered all over the evening news. This threat is usually bluster. If neither you nor your company has done anything seriously wrong, you generally have little to fear. The great majority of local investigative journalists are hardworking folks who are not out to destroy businesses or careers just because a customer is unhappy. Most of them only want to expose the shady practices of unethical businesses.

However, the threat can still be real. Not all reporters are ethical in these matters, and even the ones who do not have an axe to grind are extremely overworked. Some will simply go for the easy sensationalism and will not take the time to thoroughly fact check a story before making your business look bad. The approach to this situation is the same as in the online/BBB section mentioned earlier in this list. Find out what the customer hopes to accomplish by reporting you and try to help him accomplish it in the moment.

- **"I'll sue your butt."** One threat that every frontline rep will encounter at some point is the threat of lawsuit. Often it is just angry talk—the person got hot and spoke in the moment—and you certainly don't want to shut down every conversation in which someone brings up a lawyer or a lawsuit. However, a legal threat is a serious threat and should not be taken lightly. While you should follow your company policies and procedures in these situations, you can use the following approach to help test how serious a customer is about the threat and decide whether to end the conversation.

  Begin by taking the temperature of the customer and presenting him a choice. Assuming you've been using all your excellent communication skills up to this point, you want to let the customer know that if he continues to threaten you with legal action, you're going to have to end the conversation. *"Sir, I really want to help make this right for you, but that's the third time you've mentioned legal action. If this is becoming a legal situation, then I'll need to stop working with you and refer you to my manager. I'd love to work with you to help resolve this issue. Would you like for me to continue working to help resolve your issue, or would you prefer that I have my manager give you a call?"*

  Feel free to take that language and tailor it to your circumstances. Also, don't use the word *threat* when confronting a customer; you have a better chance of moving the conversation forward if you don't use the term.

- **"I'll kick your butt."** I've dealt with a man who demanded a cash refund on the spot and refused to leave the lobby, a grown man who threw a tantrum at a young female sales associate and stormed out saying, "This is *not* over," and a customer who violently slammed a clipboard down and shouted, "This is ridiculous," when asked to fill out a form. While overreaction to intense customers should be guarded against, physical threats should not be taken lightly. I won't speak in depth about this topic, because it's too serious an issue for a nonprofessional. I highly recommend Gavin DeBecker's book *The Gift of Fear* to understand threats in the workplace.

From the customer service side, the advice is simple: As with a true legal threat, once a physical threat is levied, the conversation is over. As a business owner, I'm no longer interested in that customer's business. As a frontline service rep, you're no longer interested in continuing the conversation and will refer the issue to management. To end the conversation, I'll let the customer know she has crossed the line by threatening me and I'm ending the conversation. Use your judgment how to do this based on the situation, but in the vast majority of circumstances, a physical threat should never be tolerated.

Being threatened is not a pleasant experience. Even lesser threats like the loss of business are inherently tough to receive because there's a part of all humans that responds on a visceral and emotional level to being threatened. Keep the smaller threats in perspective, and use the concepts discussed in this chapter to put yourself in a better position to handle threats when they come.

CHAPTER 75

What to Do When a Customer with an Audience Goes Crazy

On occasion, an angry customer will play out his personal drama on the service floor in full view of teammates and other customers. In one of my businesses, we refer to it as "a lobby meltdown." The customer might scream, yell, or cuss. The person might pitch such a fit that everyone around him stops what they're doing and either watches him or listens while avoiding eye contact with him. When a lobby meltdown occurs, it has an impact on customers in the vicinity, and it's important that you acknowledge the situation with other customers once it is over.

The difference between a Hero-Class rep and most frontline reps is in how you acknowledge it. In Chapter 40, I recommended that you never speak badly about customers in front of other customers. That principle is just as true when a customer goes crazy in front of an audience. You want to avoid reacting negatively toward the customer or the situation. Don't roll your eyes, shake your head, or make a comment like, *"What a nut job."* It's a natural reaction, but it's the wrong one. Those comments are about *you* and how *you* feel. Your job is to be concerned with the customer whose experience was just impacted. Your comments should acknowledge the situation without commenting on the person. *"I apologize that you had to witness that, Ma'am. I assure you that's not typical here."* If the circumstances are right, you can often throw in a harmless joke at the end. *"So how was the rest of your experience?"*

Often, the customers will be more offended and angry than you are. They'll try to commiserate with you by commenting on the situation. *"What a jerk. You should make sure that guy never comes back here."* Almost always, the customer means well and is in her own way trying to be supportive of you; however, you don't want to join her on a trip to negative town.

Your goal is to show appreciation while redirecting the conversation to something more productive. *"I appreciate your saying that. It happens sometimes. What's important to me is to make sure that the rest of your experience is great."* When an angry customer affects other customers, make sure your focus is on repairing the customers' experience and not on letting them make you feel better.

PART NINE

UNDERSTAND THE DIGITAL FRONT LINES

CHAPTER 76

The Channel Impacts the Message

When customer service on the phone was discussed in Chapter 46, we noted that the lack of visual cues created communication challenges not present in face-to-face interactions. Communication through digital channels is even more challenging. With digital communication, you've removed almost all of the implied messages that come through facial expression and tone of voice. Customers may be able to hear you smile over the phone, but they certainly can't via email, and typing one of these—☺—is not the same thing.

In customer service, each channel through which we communicate with customers brings its own unique characteristics to the exchange that can impact and even alter meaning. In this part of the book, I want to introduce you to some of the unique aspects of providing customer service through digital media. Since covering the entire spectrum of customer-facing digital communication would take us too far afield from our core subject matter, we'll focus on the three areas that are most likely to impact you on the front lines: privacy and security, email communication, and social media customer service.

As we work through these chapters, please keep in mind that, as we said earlier, the unique characteristics of the medium don't change the fundamental principles of customer service. The basics stay the same, even if the communication patterns need to be adapted. The goal in these next few chapters is not to make you an expert on these topics but to expose you to some core principles and techniques that will make you more effective on the digital front lines.

CHAPTER 77

Privacy and Security Are
the New Triggers

If I had to make a list of potential topics that might be worthy of being labeled the eighth Service Trigger, that list would have to include privacy and security. Both of these are hot-button issues for customers nowadays, and, accordingly, it's crucial that you respect a customer's privacy and let her know her information is secure. As you'll see in a moment, not every privacy or security issue is based on digital communications; however, I've included the topic here because so many of these issues are related to the digital arena.

Privacy is a challenging topic because customers can be a bit inconsistent in this area. On the one hand, they seem to barely care about privacy at all. Consumers willingly trade their long-term privacy for the sake of convenience and seemingly inconsequential financial benefits. They give away their information to mobile apps that track their every move, computer software that collects data on them, and in-store discount cards that keep a record of all their purchases. And, of course, many customers paste their entire lives all over the social media for the world to see. On the other hand, somewhere in each customer's mind are boundaries—ideas they have about how their personal privacy should be protected. While customers might not always be consistent on the topics of privacy and security, that should not diminish your view of how important the topic is to them. One 2010 study by Fujitsu Limited, a leading manufacturer of computing products, found that 88 percent of people are worried about who has access to their data.[1]

A story from one of my retail businesses shows just how murky the privacy waters can be. We had a couple who used to come in for appointments together frequently. They were regulars who would joke around at the front desk, and a number of our associates knew them well. One day, the husband called to see if his wife was at the business receiving a service, and an associate let him know that she was. What the sales associate hadn't noticed was that the couple had not been in together in a couple of months. Unfortunately, there was a reason for that, which the associate was not aware of: The couple was in the midst of a messy divorce. Using the information from the associate, the husband showed up at the business, confronted the wife, and began an argument with her on the sidewalk, where other customers could see. The wife wasn't happy, feeling we had violated her privacy, even though two months before she would have expected us to give the husband that same information. We managed to resolve the issue and made sure no further violations occurred, but the situation demonstrates how tricky a matter privacy can be.

When a customer believes you have violated his privacy or security, here are some strategies you can use to address those matters above and beyond the standard CATER process described in Chapter 58:

- Make sure you understand specifically what the customer is upset about.
- Emphasize how important his privacy/security is to you and the company.
- Highlight the physical systems your company has in place to protect customer privacy/security.
- Focus on the policies and procedures your company has in place to protect customer privacy/security.
- Emphasize the difference between your company's normal process and a mistake.
- Ask the customer what would make him comfortable moving forward.

Perhaps the most important thing to remember is that when a customer has concerns about privacy or security, whether preemptively or because an issue has occurred, you want to do more than just answer her questions, you want to give her confidence in your company and you. Nothing will create this confidence more than showing her that you understand and care about her concerns and then emphasizing the processes and systems you have in place to protect her going forward.

Notes

1. Fujitsu, *Personal Data in the Cloud: A Global Survey of Consumer Attitudes,* http://www.fujitsu.com/global/Images/FSL-0011_A4_Privacy Report_online_101207.pdf. Accessed September 23, 2014.

CHAPTER 78

Good Email Is an Art

Of all of the digital media frontline professionals use, email is by far the most common. Yet so many companies and reps don't put the energy and thought into their emails that they put into other customer service communication. The art of good customer service emails is multifaceted and involves good general email practices like having a strong subject line, avoiding language that trips up spam filters, and being careful of attachment size. It also involves using calculated customer-centric approaches. When using email to respond to customer issues or concerns, be sure to:

1. Employ thoughtful customer service language. Most of the communication skills we discussed in Part Six are just as relevant in an email as they are in person or on the phone. You should say "please" and "thank you." You should use power words. You should present issues through the most effective frame.

2. Use an informal tone when possible. One of the challenges on the digital front lines is connecting with the person on the other end of the exchange without facial cues and tone of voice. Using stilted, stuffy language makes your communication seem distant and insincere. On the other hand, you're not texting a friend, and you shouldn't be using poor grammar, punctuation, capitalization, or spelling. I'm not saying you should never add the occasional smiley face or use a sentence fragment, but always remain professional.

3. Incorporate repeatable elements for maximum efficiency and effectiveness. Good emails are a pain in the you know what. When you're working with a difficult situation and need to be extra careful that you leave no room for misinterpretation, emails can take time to find just the right language and the right tone. Fortunately, in customer service we often deal with similar situations, and the best thing you can do when you have effective language for a certain scenario is to save it and reuse it. This isn't about having canned responses but about having preset elements you can combine to create a customized response. Keep in mind that the same 12 notes of the chromatic scale were used to create Beethoven's Fifth Symphony and Miley Cyrus's "Party in the USA." The results are as much about how you put the parts together as what the parts are.

4. Design with details in mind. When constructing these repeatable elements and other parts of your emails, focus on the little details that can have an impact. This applies to language, graphics, and even what's in your signature block.

5. Address issues directly. Email autoresponders have their place, but when you're actually responding to an email, you never want your answer to come across as canned. The number one way for a message to seem canned is for it to not address the customer's issue directly. I'm sure you've received a response from a company that you read and thought, *"Lovely. You didn't even respond to my question."* Remember that frustration and you'll take the time to make sure your customers don't feel the same way.

6. Present options for further contact. Always leave the digital door open at the end of your emails. Assuring accountability and offering direct access to you are key. It's easy to think you've answered all the customer's questions, but you never really know for sure. Leaving the door open helps assure the customer that you're committed to a resolution.

7. Remember the human on the other side. Jeannie Walters, founder of 360Connext and my cohost on the *Crack the Customer Code* podcast, points out how easy it is to lose sight that there's a human being on the other end of these types of communication. *"If we don't remember that there are real people on the receiving end of our communications,"* she says, *"we end up dehumanizing people and situations go from bad to worse quickly."*[1]

In many ways, email is an excellent medium for customer communication. It's private, it enables you to document your conversation, and it allows you to send files and complex information. Yet, it also has its limitations. Emails are time consuming to craft in difficult situations, more open to misinterpretation than conversation, and there's a lag between responses. The more complex or difficult a situation, the less effective non-immediate response media like email are. When possible, move more challenging service issues off of email and to the phone. Clear the issue up in a conversation if possible, and use email to document the results and help prevent future misunderstandings.

Notes

1. Jeannie Walters, "Blast from the Past—It's a (REALLY, REALLY) Small World," 360Connext, July 19, 2012, http://360connext.com/blast-from-the-past-its-a-really-really-small-world/. Accessed September 23, 2014.

CHAPTER 79

The Social Customer Is
Here to Stay

You're probably aware that social media is one of the biggest changes to customer service in the last decade. As a frontline rep, you may or may not have any involvement with customers through social media. In larger companies, it tends to be delegated to dedicated teams or outside agencies, and even then customer service departments are involved less than 20 percent of the time.[1] In some smaller companies—where it's all hands on deck and service reps are also inventory checkers, bathroom cleaners, and guerrilla marketing experts—frontline reps may end up managing the company's social media presence. For those of you in this position, this chapter will introduce you to the basics of social media for customer service. For those of you who aren't, you might still want to learn more about the topic. With the current growth of social media for customer service, it's becoming relevant to more and more frontline positions every day.

Despite its current level of popularity, the use of social media for customer service continues to grow in importance. While social customer service has been around for years, we're seeing an increasing number of service interactions moving to platforms like Facebook and Twitter. One indication of this trend is the industry response. An analysis out of Europe released in 2014 found that only 38 percent of companies have integrated social media into their contact center strategies, but that number is expected to reach 63 percent in 2016.[2] Companies go where the customers are, and that is increasingly social media. Nothing I've seen suggests that the social customer service trend will slow down anytime soon.

For customer service, social media matters, and what customers say and do on social media has to be paid attention to. Social media has changed the way many customers interact with companies and have given each individual customer a more powerful voice. While there has been a bit of hysteria around how powerful any individual voice is, this does not mean that the online voice of the customer is not important. Every online comment has an impact, and one thing you should remember as you work with customers through social media is that negative comments have an even greater impact. One study found that a single negative experience posted in public could negate five positive ones.[3] Regardless of whether the interaction is positive, neutral, or negative, staying on top of social customer service interactions is important to companies of all sizes.

For purposes of this discussion, I'll use the term "social media" broadly to include not only obvious channels like Twitter, Facebook, and Google+, but also any online channel where people socially interact with companies or each other. That means sites like Google reviews, Yelp, and TripAdvisor. While there are nuances to each type of channel and how you handle customer service responses, I want to leave you with some basic principles that are generally applicable when communicating through customers via all these channels:

- **Monitor your brand on social media.** In addition to monitoring your own channels, use third-party services to monitor what's being said in other online venues. Google Alerts is the standard, but communications expert Gini Dietrich recommends Talkwalker alerts as a "more efficient" alternative.[4] Talkwalker seems to catch some things that Google Alerts doesn't.
- **Don't panic.** It can be difficult to see an unpleasant comment show up on social media. Take a deep breath and remember that people who read the review or comment are looking to see how you respond. When someone says your company is rude and unprofessional, you want the tone and character of your response to give the opposite impression.

- **Follow the CATER process (see Chapter 58).** For negative comments, follow your standard complaint handling process. Just keep it brief and to the point.
- **Prepare canned lines.** As with email, you want preset, reusable material at the ready. The difference on social media is that everyone can see your responses, so even with effective language you can still seem canned if you're saying the same thing to every person. The key is to have a lot of premade phrases at your disposal so you can mix things up. On Twitter this can be a challenge because of space limitations, which is why it's important to put some thought into it ahead of time.
- **Respond consistently.** Whether comments are positive or negative, responses are important. This doesn't always mean you have to respond to every comment. There are some situations where you might not, but in general if someone takes the time to comment, you should respond.
- **Respond promptly.** Social media is immediate, and customers often resort to social channels because they think it will get them a quicker response or a response at all. One study by Edison Research done for The Social Habit website showed that 42 percent of consumers expect a response to social media within 60 minutes.[5] The only way to be prepared for expectations like that is to have preset guidelines for responses and make sure your channels are actively monitored.
- **Never, ever respond with anger or sarcasm.** Social media channels are no different in this regard from other customer service channels, except that if you lose your cool or communicate in an unprofessional manner, it will be out there for the world to see.
- **Take it offline.** While social media can be great for quick service issues or pointing a customer in the right direction, it's a terrible way to handle difficult or complicated customer service issues. It's short form, it's completely devoid of human signals, and, yes, it's public. From Chapter 20, we know how

much customers hate being transferred, so when possible, try to resolve the customer's issue via the channel she used to contact you. For more complicated situations, do your best to take it offline as soon as possible. Have preset phrases ready to go to help move the conversation to a more constructive medium.

The above list just scratches the surface, but it should give you some sound principles to follow so you approach social customer service more effectively. Just bear in mind that this is a rich topic that requires much more than a single chapter to explore thoroughly.

Notes

1. Jeremy Taylor, "15 Social Customer Service Statistics," May 28, 2013, Sentiment, http://www.sentimentmetrics.com/blog/2013/05/28/15 -social-customer-service-statistics/. Accessed September 23, 2014.

2. Sam Heggie-Collins, *Social Media to Significantly Increase in Contact Centre Strategies,* September 2014, http://www.contactcentre news.co.uk/2014/09/02/social-media-to-significantly-increase-in-contact-centre-strategies/. Accessed October 27, 2014.

3. NM Incite, *State of Social Customer Service 2012,* http://soulofbrands .files.wordpress.com/2012/11/nm-incite-report-the-state-of-social -customer-service-2012.pdf. Accessed September 23, 2014.

4. Gini Dietrich, *Spin Sucks: Communication and Reputation Management in the Digital Age* (Que Publishing, 2014), Kindle ed., ch. 9, sec.: "Create a Strategy," loc. 2691.

5. Jay Baer, "Are Consumer Expectations for Social Customer Service Realistic?," Social Habit, http://sociahabit.com/uncategorized/cus tomer-service-expectations/. Accessed September 23, 2014.

PART TEN

BE YOUR CUSTOMER'S HERO

CHAPTER **80**

What Really Makes a Hero-Class Customer Experience?

We've come a long way together so far, and I hope you've learned a lot that will help you succeed in a customer-facing role. In this last part, I want to help pull all the pieces together for you and look at what it really takes to be your customer's hero.

The question this chapter asks is simple: What really makes a Hero-Class customer experience? The answer, as you might suspect, is much more complicated. For those who work at the strategic level of customer experience, what makes customers loyal is an age-old debate. Industry websites, specific research methodologies, and entire books are dedicated to promoting this theory or that, or to explaining which theories work in what contexts. If you don't follow these discussions, you might wonder what they could be debating. After all, customer service is pretty simple, right?

Actually, the customer-centered disciplines can be incredibly complex. Here are just a few of the hotly debated questions in the fields of customer experience and customer service:

- What's more important for creating customer loyalty, delivering amazing experiences or effortless experiences?
- Does a positively resolved customer service issue make a customer more loyal than having no issue at all?

- What's the single best indicator of future customer loyalty —a customer who says she is satisfied or one who says she'll recommend your company to a friend?

There is disagreement among very smart people about all of those questions.

While this book is not the place to explore these theories or even to defend those I subscribe to, I mention the lack of agreement so you'll know that the theory of Hero-Class customer service that I've presented throughout this book and that I'll focus on in this part is by no means the gospel of customer service. It's what I believe based on the available research and my own experience. To paraphrase the Marine Corps' Rifleman's Creed: *This is my theory. There are many like it, but this one is mine.*

It is tempting to be seduced by the lofty language of customer service—my own included. Terms like *amazement, delight*, and *Hero-Class* tend to get associated with over-the-top acts of service. However, most sober professionals who embrace these terms do so through a practical, real-world lens. I can think of no better examples than my colleagues Shep Hyken and Steve Curtin, who have made amazement and delight respectively centerpieces of their service messaging.

In his book *The Amazement Revolution,* Shep says Amazement is "Service that is consistently and predictably better than average. Amazement is not necessarily about 'Wow!' levels of service, although sometimes it may be. It is about an all-of-the-time, I-know-I-can-count-on-it, better-than-average experience."[1] Steve says it similarly in his book *Delight Your Customers*: "This book is not about how to 'WOW!' customers by continually surpassing their expectations and exceeding their needs—which is unsustainable. . . . In everyday service situations, most customers simply want to be acknowledged and appreciated."[2]

I could not agree with these statements more. In my view, customer loyalty does not require elaborate philosophies or complicated ideas. You need only three elements to create a Hero-Class customer experience and to keep customers loyal:

1. Meet and, whenever possible, exceed expectations.
2. Provide a hassle-free, frictionless experience.
3. Do both of the above consistently.

Meeting or exceeding expectations is the baseline for all great customer experiences. If you fail to hit the mark on what the customer expects, then the experience won't be memorable or positive. To begin, you must do everything you can to know what the customer expects—on a personal level when possible and on a general level when not. Exceeding expectations is not about creating over-the-top experiences. You can exceed expectations by delivering a product a day early or carrying an item out to someone's car. You can exceed expectations by being hyperattentive and communicating thoroughly. You can exceed expectations by following up with customers and proactively checking in on them. You don't have to provide lavish extras or viral-worthy experiences for each customer; you just do your job with a smile, do it well, and make sure you give your customers a little more than they expect whenever possible.

You also want to create hassle-free, frictionless experiences. I spoke in Chapter 18 about the concept of customer effort and how important it is to be easy to do business with. Customers simply want their interactions with your company and you to be as easy as possible. The Hero-Class rep is always looking for ways to make the customer's journey smooth and hassle free. Whether it's removing bureaucracy, preparing forms in advance for a customer, or attempting to preemptively resolve issues or anticipating problems, making the customer's experience as easy as it can be will separate your company from the competition and distinguish you from your colleagues on the service floor.

Finally, I believe that "consistency is the greatest WOW of all."[3] Consistency creates a sense of dependability, and even more than that it creates a sense of trust. One study found that of the three factors that matter to establishing trust in economic relationships— the frequency of interaction, the competence of the trustee, and the consistency of the trustee—"the consistency of the trustee's previous behavior is the most important element in engendering . . . trust."[4] When you think about what creates trust, it's dependability, and in customer service, that comes from consistently being there for the customer when you're supposed to be and delivering what she's looking for.

Providing Hero-Class customer service begins and ends with the fundamentals. Don't allow yourself to get distracted. There will always be a new story of over-the-top customer service; there will always be an author or speaker (myself included) telling you how the Ritz-Carlton hotel or Zappos.com does this or that. Let these stories inspire you, but don't let them discourage you. Consistently meet or exceed your customer's expectations with experiences that are hassle free, and you'll become the customer's hero each and every time.

Notes

1. Shep Hyken, *The Amazement Revolution* (Greenleaf Book Group, 1st ed., 2011), Kindle edition, 2.

2. Steve Curtin, *Delight Your Customers: 7 Simple Ways to Raise Your Customer Service from Ordinary to Extraordinary* (AMACOM, 2013), Kindle edition, 4.

3. Adam Toporek, *7 Secret Customer Service Techniques . . . Every Expert Knows* (CTS Service Solutions, 2014), ebook, 2nd ed., 6.

4. Paul Dunn, "The Importance of Consistency in Establishing Cognitive-Based Trust: A Laboratory Experiment," *Teaching Business Ethics* 4, no. 3 (August 2000), http://link.springer.com/article/10.1023% 2FA%3A1009870417073. Accessed September 23, 2014.

CHAPTER 81

Adopt the Mindset of a Hero

This book began with the idea that great service is all in your head, and now we've come full circle, because the most important thing you'll need to implement the tips and techniques you've learned is to adopt the mindset of a hero. Having a Hero-Class mindset means that you have a desire to serve the customer and make her happy and that you're willing to do what it takes to make that happen. Of course, *you* have this desire; if you didn't, you never would've made it through the 80 chapters that preceded this one. But it bears mentioning that the techniques in this book will have limited effectiveness if they're not used by a rep who has a genuine desire to serve. It's the combination of skill, judgment, and attitude that makes a service rep Hero-Class.

Adopting a Hero-Class mindset also involves the ability to keep failure in perspective. As you begin integrating these tips and techniques into your customer care, you're going to fail on occasion. Either the technique itself won't work, or you'll fail to execute it properly. The key is not to let yourself get rattled when this happens, and not to let yourself lose faith in the techniques.

There will always be a time when a technique that works 99 percent of the time simply doesn't. Say you decide to try using your authority, which you learned in Chapter 65. You walk over to a customer, warmly extend your hand, and introduce yourself as the shift supervisor. The customer replies, in a biting, sarcastic tone, "Is that supposed to impress me?" It's harsh, it's cutting, and it's not something you want to feel again. Yet, you can't let these types of one-off situations make you hesitant to use the technique in the future. As we discussed in Chapter 14, the same mechanism that teaches us not to touch a hot stove also helps us create all sorts of false associations. Don't let the failure of a technique make you think it doesn't work. When used at the right time and in the right way, these techniques do work, and work well.

Sometimes the problem is not the technique but the execution. On occasion, you're going to mess up, and that's okay. Remember, a lot of this is not natural. It's a skill you have to learn, just like playing the guitar or programming a computer. The more you practice, the better you'll get. Don't let yourself get flustered when you don't hit the ball out of the park every time at bat.

Finally, I want you to keep in mind that customer service is messy and sometimes unrewarding. As discussed in the Introduction, no matter how great a customer experience you deliver, it will not always prevent customers from being disappointed. The secret sauce of this book is found in the fact that if you use the tips and techniques regularly and adopt the mindset of a hero, you'll prevent and preempt a host of problems. You'll also ensure that mild issues never escalate into huge disputes. If you put the tips and techniques you've learned in this book into practice consistently, you'll discover one simple fact: Being your customer's hero pays off.

CHAPTER 82

Be Your Customer's Hero

Why should you want to be your customer's hero? What exactly is the point? We've briefly touched on how delivering Hero-Class customer service can make your job more fulfilling, but I don't think we've done the concept justice. As I considered the final message I wanted you to leave this book with, I kept coming back to one thing:

It feels good to deliver exceptional customer experiences; it feels great to be your customer's hero.

To be your customer's hero means to make his day a little easier and to put a smile on his face. To be your customer's hero means to solve her problem and lessen her stress. To be your customer's hero means to decrease his anxiety and make him feel appreciated. Put simply, to be your customer's hero means you've had a positive, noticeable impact on your customer's day.

When you do these things for your customer, you'll be rewarded too. You'll have less stress and more fun, you'll deal with fewer problems and solve many more, and you'll feel more confident and more appreciated. When you become your customer's hero, it's as good an experience for you as it is for her. Brightening someone else's day simply feels good.

Delivering Hero-Class customer service is not easy. It takes effort, it takes foresight, and it takes practice, but the rewards are well worth it. I can only hope that one day I'll step onto your service floor and you'll use the tips and techniques in this book to be my hero.

Putting What You've
Learned into Practice

This book covers a wide range of customer service concepts and techniques. There's a lot to absorb, and the inevitable question once you've reached the end is, "Where do I start?" To help you answer this question, I want to give you a couple of quick tips for putting what you've learned into practice.

First, focus on the fundamentals, particularly those in Parts Four through Six. A host of the foundational techniques we covered in those middle parts are applicable across all types of service situations. Being familiar with these techniques will pay off in low-pressure and high-pressure customer situations.

Next, don't try to eat the entire buffet in one meal. Pick the parts that resonate with you most and then use the 80/20 rule (or Pareto Principle) to work those first. In this context, the 80/20 rule would mean that 80 percent of your results would come from 20 percent of the techniques you master. Find the vital few techniques you think will really pay off in your situation and concentrate on those.

Finally, to thank you for reading *Be Your Customer's Hero* and for allowing me to be part of your professional journey, I've created a free PDF workbook to help you through the process of putting what you've learned into practice. The workbook will allow you to home in on the skills that will be of the most value to you on the service floor. To download it, simply go to customers thatstick.com/free-hero-workbook/ and type "hero2015" in the password field. When you download your free workbook, you'll also begin to receive our free e-newsletter, *The Customer Conversation*, which will give you a number of free resources that can help you grow even further in your customer-facing role.

Yours in service,
Adam Toporek

Index